CREATION SPEAKS

Devotions Based on God's First Book of Revelation

By

Jerry Lang

Chapbook Press

Schuler Books
2660 28th Street SE
Grand Rapids, MI 49512
(616) 942-7330
www.schulerbooks.com

Creation Speaks: Devotions Based on God's First Book of Revelation

ISBN 13: 9781957169378

Library of Congress Control Number: 2023903079

The following devotions previously appeared in slightly different form in various editions of *The Secret Place* between 2011 and 2021: "Pine Praises," "Changing Perspectives," "Extravagant Grace," "Snowshoes," "Old Bean Plants," "Beautiful Feet," "Church in the Park," "Woodland Pastels," "Delight in Wisdom," "Blue Sky," and "Lightning."

"Weed Bouquets" (Wild Flowers and Weeds) appeared in *The Upper Room*, May-June 2011.

Printed in the United States by Chapbook Press.

For Alison

The heavens proclaim the glory of God;
the skies proclaim the work of his hands.
Day after day they pour forth speech;
night after night they display knowledge.

Psalm 19:1-2

I would like to thank Ali Koomen and Phillip Sterling for their time and effort editing and proofreading these devotions. I especially thank Phillip for his invaluable help in formatting the book.

I give special thanks to my wife, Alison, for reviewing and commenting on many of the devotions and for being a steadfast prayer partner for over half a century. I also would like to thank several friends who spent time reading and commenting on the devotions.

Contents:

Creation Speaks

INTRODUCTION

The diversity of life, the mysteries hidden in the Earth, and the unfathomable expanse of the universe speak of an all-powerful and creative God. God expresses Himself in uncountable ways through His creation. As Paul states in Romans 20, "For since the creation of the world God's invisible qualities—His eternal power and divine nature—have been clearly seen, being understood from what has been made, so that men are without excuse."

In attempting to learn about God and His role in our lives, most Christians rely on Scripture which, as stated in 2 Timothy 3:16. is "God-breathed and is useful for teaching, rebuking, correcting and training in righteousness . . ." While Scripture is the bedrock of our Christian faith, there are also clues to our understanding of God in the types of bedrock beneath our feet, in the plants and animals with whom we share this planet, and in the starlight streaming to us from light-years away.

Just as with learning Scripture, learning from the "book of nature" takes prayer, patience, and persistence. Spending quiet times in prayer outdoors often allows the Holy Spirit to speak clearly to the heart.

These devotions are based on everyday observations of God's creation seen through Scripture-informed (but not theologically trained) eyes. Creation can "speak" of the Lord and for the Lord anywhere.

This book is arranged with five devotions for each week of the year. At the end of each five, there is a suggestion for you to use your own creativity in getting closer to God through His creation and/or through your actions and perceptions. Use these devotions and suggestions anyway you wish any day you wish and any season you wish.

Most of the Scripture quotes are from the New International Version of the Bible. If other versions were used, they are noted at the end of each quote.

My hope is that these devotions encourage you to grow in faith and begin or continue your own explorations of finding the fingerprints of God throughout His wondrous creation. In your observations and wanderings, may you say as did Samuel, "Speak Lord, for your servant is listening." (1 Samuel 3:9)

JANUARY DEVOTIONS

Contents:

Week 1 /Day 1

THE MANY NAMES FOR SNOW

For to us a child is born, to us a son is given, and the government will be on His shoulders. And He will be called Wonderful Counselor, Mighty God, Everlasting Father, Prince of Peace. Isaiah 9:6

The Inuit, Aivilik, and Igloolik languages have over 30 words for snow. These native peoples of the Arctic are intimately familiar with all the various forms, textures, colors, and properties of snow since they depend on this kind of knowledge for winter survival. In contrast, the English language is rather poor in its vocabulary related to snow. Any further descriptions beyond "snow" are accomplished by adding adjectives such as *slushy, heavy,* or *powdery.*
The differences among languages in describing the finer nuances of something often reflect the importance of an object or phenomenon to those using the language.

Many names throughout the Bible are applied to Jesus. In English these include *Messiah, Lord, Son of Man, Son of God, Immanuel, King of Kings, Rabbi, Lamb of God,* and many others. To the non-believer, Jesus may be only a historical figure with one name, but to the believer who has experienced the life-changing aspects of giving their lives to Jesus, He becomes much more. He meets us at our need by whatever name is required: *Counselor, Comforter, Lamb of God, Savior, Creator, Redeemer, King,* or by a thousand other names. Call on Him today.

Week 1 /Day 2

LEAVING IMPRESSIONS

I will bless the Lord at all times; his praise shall continually be in my mouth. My soul shall make its <u>boast</u> in the Lord. The humble shall hear of it and be glad. Oh, magnify the Lord with me, and let us exalt his name together. Psalm 34:1-3 NKJV

I was walking along a snowy trail through the woods on a bright sunny afternoon last February. The snow had been on the ground for days, and a few late-falling maple and oak leaves were laying on top of snow along the trail. I noticed that the leaves appeared somewhat sunken into the snow. When I picked one up, I saw that the darker leaf had absorbed more of the sun's heat than did the surrounding snow, and it had melted a very distinct impression of its shape into the snow.

As Christians, our lives need to be warmed by the power of the Holy Spirit so that we can leave an impression of God's love in the world. We can influence the world around us for God by letting His grace empower us. Let's make an impression for the Lord on the world around us by tapping into the power of the Holy Spirit and exhibiting the fruits of the Spirit in our lives (Galatians 5:22).

Week 1 /Day 3

BURNING BUSHES

"Do not come any closer," God said. "Take off your sandals for the place you are standing is holy ground." Exodus 3:5

The extensive wetlands and a creek near my Michigan home is ideal habitat for red osier dogwood—a beautiful native shrub. In a winter landscape filled with brown and gray tones on a background of white, this little shrub stands out with its bright red stems that seem to glow from within. Although it may not actually be on fire as with Moses' burning bush (Exodus 3:1-10), the warm, red coloration of the dogwood stems continually "burn" in the dull winter landscape.

The red dogwood stems can be a reminder of how promise can appear in the midst of the unpromising. In God's presence, we might think we are just standing on frozen wasteland, but He calls us to revere it as holy ground—a place of promise and of God's spirit (Exodus 3:5).

All ground is holy ground. Be ready to listen for God's promises in your life regardless of the appearance of your surroundings. Look for burning bushes. Through the working of the Holy Spirit, you will see them where others see nothing but a scraggly plant, even if it has red stems!

Week 1 /Day 4

ICING OVER

They all joined together constantly in prayer, along with the women and Mary the mother of Jesus and with his brothers. Acts 1:14

There were several weeks of very cold weather last winter. During that time, I took daily walks along a small creek near our house. The creek had small riffles where the water flowed over rocks. As the days of subfreezing temperatures continued, ice began forming along the banks and around the larger rocks where the water was quieter. These shelves of ice continued to expand inch-by-inch into more rapidly moving water until finally, after several weeks, even the riffles were frozen over.

Of all the practices needed to maintain a strong faith, prayer is the most important. Even so, it is often pushed to the periphery of our lives while we busy ourselves with good works and Christian fellowship.

Is ice forming along the edges of your faith life? If so, melt it away with the fire of the Holy Spirit through prayer.

Week 1 /Day 5

NORTH WOODS SPIRES

I press on toward the goal to win the prize for which God has called me heavenward in Christ Jesus. Philippians 3:14

Black spruce trees are perfectly designed to withstand the rigors of northern winters. Accumulated snow and ice can place a heavy load on deciduous trees like maples and oaks and can often break off branches. The spruce trees' narrow pointed profiles and pliable branches of thin, slippery needles easily shed such loads. The growth habit of these trees is focused on upward rather than lateral growth.

As Christians we also need focus in our spiritual growth. As recounted in Luke 9:62, Jesus reminds us that once we place our hands on the plow to follow Him, we need never look back. The civil rights-era folk song, "Keep Your Eyes on the Prize" was based on this biblical passage. The spiritual "I Have Decided to Follow Jesus" based on Luke 9:57 also encourages Kingdom focus— "the cross before me, the world behind me".

Trusting in Jesus will give us a life where worries and cares slide off like snow from a black spruce. While our pliable branches of care and compassion for others reach out around us as we grow in Christ, we maintain our heavenward focus pressing on to the prize.

This Coming Week

Ask yourself at the end of each day: By what name have you known Him best today?

Week 2 /Day 1

CLOUD SHAPES AND THEOPHANIES

And just as He was coming up out of the water, He saw the heavens torn apart and the Spirit descending like a dove on Him. Mark 1:10

Showers and thunderstorms drifted around southern Arizona one Sunday morning late in January. As my wife and I left church, we were fascinated by the beautiful cloud formations. White cottony cumulus and scattered dark-bottomed cumulonimbus clouds scudded over a partially exposed canvas of blue sky.

The changing cloud formations were so dramatic that my wife grabbed her camera out of the car to take a few shots from the church parking lot. When we later examined the photos, we were surprised by what we saw—a cloud formation appearing very much like a winged dove over the church steeple!

In the Bible, clouds are often associated with the presence and activity of God: A "pillar of cloud" guided the Israelites (Exodus 13:21); Moses ascended into the clouds of Mount Sinai to meet with God (Exodus 24:16); and the Lord's presence was described as "a cloud over the tabernacle in the temple" (Numbers 9:15; 1 Kings 8:10-11). The Transfiguration of Jesus also took place within a cloud on the mountain (Mark 9:7), and Jesus is expected to return "on the clouds" (Revelation 14:14).

Was the cloud over the church a visible manifestation of the Holy Spirit, or was it just a meteorological happenstance? I tend to believe the first, for God sightings are only visible through the eyes of faith. As Elizabeth Barrett Browning so aptly stated, "Earth's crammed with heaven, / And every common bush afire with God; / But only he who sees, takes off his shoes, /The rest sit round it and pluck blackberries." Keep your eyes and ears open in faith. God still appears and speaks!

Week 2 /Day 2

ORION

I have loved you with an everlasting love; I have drawn you with loving-kindness. Jeremiah 31:3

As the days shorten, my early morning walks in the fall become more like walking in the middle of the night. During these walks, I often observe the constellation Orion, The Hunter, in the predawn sky. Orion's belt of three stars in a line along with several bright surrounding stars makes the constellation easy to find among the myriad of other stars.

Although Orion is a character from Greek and Roman mythology, the constellation is mentioned three times in the Bible (Job 9:9; Job 38:31-32; Amos 5:8). God's power of creating the constellations and having power over them is clearly outlined in these passages. Like Orion, God is also a hunter—not of some mythological animal but rather of our souls. He continually calls out to bring us in range of His love.

Orion is most visible during the darker seasons of the year, the seasons traditionally associated with hunting (fall and winter), just as the brightness of God's presence is often most visible during our personally darkest hours. Yet, Orion is present somewhere in the sky in the warmer months as well, just as God's presence is also always with us. We don't have to wait until darkness falls to respond to His call and let The Hunter capture our souls.

Week 2 /Day 3

THE CROW CHOIR

My mouth will speak in praise of the Lord. Let every creature praise his holy name forever and ever. Psalm 145:21

Most people would agree that crows are not the most beautiful of birds and that their cawing is less than melodic. Farmers in some areas consider them pests. However, despite their shortcomings, crows are smart birds and reportedly care for one another in social groups. What I like most about crows is that although they may not be great singers, they belt it out year-round. Unlike many songbirds, you can count on hearing crows in any season. Crows follow the guidance of Psalm 145:21 every day, "Let every creature praise His holy name."

I've heard many people in church say they don't sing or can't sing hymns and praise songs because they can't carry a tune. That never bothers crows, and it shouldn't bother us either when we "make a joyful noise to the Lord" (Psalm 100:1). We should be ready "in season and out of season" (2 Timothy 4:2) to not only sing our praises to the Lord, but to show the world that the joy of the Lord overflows in us no matter what the season of our life. Let's join the crows in singing our Creator's praises. We truly have something to crow about—the love of Jesus! The world needs to hear it.

Week 2 /Day 4

A GLACIALLY SLOW REBOUND

He will wipe every tear from their eyes. There will be no more death or mourning or crying or pain, for the old order of things has passed away. Revelation 21:4

During the last period of the Ice Age, glacial ice up to a mile thick slowly ground across the Midwest. The slow-moving ice gouged out softer soil, gravel, and rock and piled it up in moraines or deposited it across the landscape as till. The landscape of the Upper Midwest, including the Great Lakes themselves, is largely a result of this ice sculpting.

Once the massive glaciers retreated northward and the tremendous weight of the glacial ice lifted from the land, the underlying bedrock began to very slowly rebound. The Niagara Escarpment, which extends in a northward arc from New York State to eastern Wisconsin, continues this rebound even today. Superior, Wisconsin, one of the towns along the escarpment, rises about one-half inch in elevation each year.

When we recognize our brokenness, confess Christ as our personal Savior, and ask for forgiveness, the weight of sin is lifted. However, our rebound from our past may be glacially slow, and we may never see full restoration in our lifetime. Residual effects in the form of broken relationships, lost financial resources, or physical problems can remain. Just as Jesus' death and resurrection did not immediately end sin in the world, so our acceptance of Christ as Savior may not immediately end the impact of past events in our lives. Yet, through continued faith in Christ, one day our complete recovery will occur—in the New Jerusalem, where our Risen Lord will reign and will wipe away every tear (Revelation 21:4).

Week 2/Day 5

SECOND BLOOM OF SNOW

We were therefore buried with Him through baptism into death in order that, just as Christ was raised from the dead through the glory of the Father, we too may live a new life. Romans 6:4

I enjoy growing sedum flowers in our garden. These are slow-growing plants with tough succulent leaves that eventually reward the gardener toward fall with some beautiful, vividly colored flowers on tightly arranged heads. Sedum stems and flower heads are very sturdy and hold their shape even after they are killed by a fall frost. Although I usually cut off or break off the old flowers in the late fall, one year I left them standing in the garden.

On a dreary winter morning a few months later, I looked out the window and saw that a gentle wet snow had piled white tufts on top of each of the dead sedum flower heads. There had been an overnight transition, leaving beautiful white winter "flowers" in the garden.

My "flowers" made me think of how Jesus is in the transformation business in our lives. With His mercy and grace falling gently on us like a pure white snowfall, He can transform our deadened spiritual lives, unfulfilled dreams, or broken bodies into something beautiful that transcends the surrounding world (Titus 3:4-6). All we need to do is accept His love, and our lives can be made beautiful.

This Coming Week

If the weather permits, go outside and view the night sky. This is best done away from city lights. Try to find the constellation Orion. Think about the timelessness of God's heavens. You are seeing the same stars as written about in the Book of Job—thought to be the oldest book in the Bible.

Week 3 /Day 1

THE RARITY OF RED

These are they who have come out of great tribulation; they have washed their robes and made them white in the blood of the Lamb. Revelation 7:14

In the animal kingdom, red is used sparingly, in comparison to the many shades of white, brown, gray, and black. Only a few beetles, moths, and butterflies are red or have red markings. A few bird species have red markings (most frequently in males, which often are important in courtship behavior), and a few like male cardinals and vermillion flycatchers are extravagantly red—they are exceptions. An occasional fish species, such as sticklebacks and red-eared sunfish, have red markings (as with the birds, it plays a role in breeding behavior). Mammals also have very little in the way of red markings.

In human culture, red catches our attention—perhaps because it's the color of our blood. As such, red is used for the lights of emergency vehicles, it's the color of fire trucks, it means stop at traffic lights, and it's given a general interpretation of warning or danger.

Biblically, red is a color associated with specialness—as in the use of red-dyed ram skins for the Tabernacle (Exodus 35:7, 23) or red horses in the visions of Zechariah. Red is also associated with warning—the warhorse of Revelation 6:4 and the dragon in Revelation 12:3.

The red that needs to catch our attention as Christians is the red of Christ's blood shed for us. As the old hymn says, "There's power in the blood of the Lamb." This gift from God can cleanse our crimson sins. The blood of Jesus has an everlasting specialness, and it also carries a warning. As Jesus clearly stated at the Last Supper, unless we drink of the cup of His blood, we cannot have everlasting life (John 6:53-58).

Week 3 /Day 2

SILVER RIBBONS IN THE DESERT

He will be like a tree planted by the water that sends out its roots by the stream. I do not fear when heat comes; its leaves are always green. It has no worries in a year of drought and never fails to bear fruit. Jeremiah 17:8

Last winter our family took a scenic train trip through the Verde Valley in central Arizona. The tall thin cottonwoods lining the Verde Riverbanks took on an icy silver glow in the slant of the afternoon sunlight. It was as if the river was lined with silver ribbons. What beauty God conveys even through the bare branches of cottonwoods!

As I viewed these shimmering silver ribbons, I thought of how the cottonwoods were not only watered by the river, but their intertwined root systems shared the life-giving water and helped the trees support and protect one another.

In Isaiah 44:4, God promises that Israel's chosen descendants will "spring up like poplar trees by flowing streams". As believers in Christ, we also are planted along God's life-giving river amidst the dry desert of the world without Him. We are nurtured by the living waters of Jesus (Psalm1:3), and we have every reason to rejoice as do the forests (Isaiah 44:2).

As we send our roots deeply into God's Word and His love, we are also called to stand beside and support each other in Christian community just as the cottonwoods along the river. Living in this way reflects 'Sonlight' to all who pass by.

Week 3 /Day 3

APOGEE AND PERIGEE

But as for me, it is good to be near God. Psalm 73:28

Earth's orbit around the Sun is elliptical rather than circular, which causes annual variations in the distance between the Sun and Earth. At apogee, the Sun-to-Earth distance is approximately 94 million miles, and at perigee the distance is about 91.5 million miles. Perigee occurs in early January, when the weather in the Northern Hemisphere is the coldest. This makes us 2.5 million miles closer to the Sun in the dark of northern winter than in the middle of a hot July day.

At times in my faith walk I feel like the psalmists who expressed anger and impatience with an uncaring and distant God (Psalm 10:1; 22:1; 42:9; 44:23-24; 74:1,11; and 79:10). It's then that I remind myself that our relationship to God has no apogee or perigee. Even in the dark hours of our nights, God is always near. He is near us no matter what warmth or coldness we seem to feel. As Paul reassures us in Philippians 4:5, with the knowledge of His nearness, we can leave all anxiety behind and replace it instead with joy and thanksgiving.

Week 3 /Day 4

CLINGING DEAD LEAVES

Generations come, and generations go, but the Earth remains forever. Ecclesiastes 1:4

My wife and I love to hike through the local parks near our Michigan home regardless of the season. On a recent early winter hike through the woods, we noticed that American beech trees were holding on to their dead leaves.

I read an article that suggested the dead leaves persisting on beech trees may have some protective role. Apparently, the leaves are bitter tasting (I never tried one!), and they may protect the beech tree's twigs and buds from hungry deer and other animals throughout the winter. In a sense, this is one generation of leaves protecting and nurturing the next generation even after death.

Like the beech leaves, Christians are called to care for God's creation both now and for future generations. Loving our neighbor extends beyond our brief lifetimes. Part of our job as Christians is to leave future generations a more just, loving, and healthful world, in which they may live and grow in their love for God and each other. (Micah 6:8).

Week 3 /Day 5

UNIVERSAL SILENCE

Be still and know that I am God. Psalm 46:10

Did you ever think about how we can only hear sound if there is some sort of atmosphere, such as the air surrounding Earth? Most of the airless universe is silent. The thermonuclear explosions on the Sun and the stars create no sound in the absence of an atmosphere. Silence accompanies the movement of the Earth around the Sun at more than 65,000 mph. All the planets, comets, asteroids, stars, and galaxies speed through the vastness of space in complete silence.

Sometimes we think God can be awfully silent Himself. But I wonder if that is because we're never quiet enough to listen. We're used to noise here on Earth and within our Western culture. We're uncomfortable with silence in conversation, and many people try to fill any silent space with radio, TV, music, and any background noise when they are alone. Our world is filled with loud music, flashing electronic images, and constant jabbering.

The Bible has many references to not being wordy in prayer or surrounding yourself with noise. The Teacher in Ecclesiastes 5:2 admonishes to "let your words be few in the presence of God." Elijah only heard God's voice in the stillness of the cave where he was hiding, rather than in the strong wind, earthquake, or fire. Quieting ourselves, and quieting our minds in contemplative prayer, should be an important part of our daily prayer life. Instead of pounding on heaven's door with our prayer requests, let's take time to sit and listen for God in silence as Mary sat and listened at Jesus' feet (Luke. 10:39).

This Coming Week

Read an article about the involvement of youth around the world pressing for more political action to address climate change.

Week 4 /Day 1

SHADOWS

He who dwells in the shelter of the Most High will rest in the shadow of the Almighty. Psalm 91:1

Shadows are often associated with something vaguely ominous or sad. Phrases like "shadowy figures," "hidden in the shadows," and "casting a shadow" all connote negative meanings.

Outdoors, shadows continually change as the seasons unfold. The long shadows of winter when the Sun is low accompany the seemingly never-ending bitter cold days. Conversely, the short shadows of summer when the Sun is almost directly overhead at noon can make us feel that there is little refuge from the heat.

Shadows denote both good and bad in the Bible. There's the "shadow of death" we so often hear about in Psalm 23, or how our lives are likened to fleeting shadows. However, there is also abiding protection in the "shadow of His wings" mentioned many times in Psalms (17:8, 36:7, 57:1, 63:7).

Be assured that we have nothing to fear from shadows in our lives if we walk in the light of God's love. He is always with us, and as the hymn "Great is Thy Faithfulness" states, "There is no shadow of turning with Thee." His love, help and protection are always available.

Week 4 /Day 2

BEAUTY INSIDE THE MOUNTAIN

Man looks at the outward appearance, but the Lord looks at the heart. 1 Samuel 16:7

My wife and I recently visited the Bisbee Mining and Historical Museum in Bisbee, Arizona. One of the exhibits in the museum highlights the beautiful minerals that were discovered by miners as they mined copper ore from the surrounding mountains. These crystallized minerals took on beautiful shapes and magnificent colors, from iridescent blues and greens to reds, pinks, and whites. I can't imagine what it must have been like for a miner to have broken into hidden rooms inside the Earth and suddenly been surrounded by a crystalline wonderland.

As with many things in creation, God has hidden beauty for us to discover. In many of us, that beauty becomes hidden under layers of hurt, rejection, anger, and sin. Yet regardless of whatever kind of spiritual overburden we accumulate, a divine spark of God is within us. Jesus could see hidden beauty in the troubled people who came to Him seeking healing and peace. As Christians, we must try to see what Jesus sees and in the way He sees, with the mining tools of compassion and love. Using these, we can break through to see the crystalline beauty hidden under even the hardest of human rocks.

Week 4 /Day 3

BITING MY TONGUE

All kinds of animals, birds, reptiles and creatures of the sea are being tamed and have been tamed by man, but no man can tame the tongue. James 2:7

One evening during dinner recently, I bit my tongue so hard that it bled. It took over a week for it to heal completely. For several days afterward, any venture into eating or drinking caused severe bolts of pain. This little incident reminded me that I eat too fast, and that I approach eating like many other things in life—hurry through them to get to the next thing.

Perhaps eating more slowly and mindfully would help me be aware of what I put into my body (a temple of the Holy Spirit) and how grateful we should be for God's provision of soil, water, and adequate Sun for crop growth. Mindful eating helps keep us aware of the human and environmental costs of producing, harvesting, and shipping the food we buy.

This little incident also made me think about the discussion of the human tongue in Chapter 3 of the Book of James. James describes the human tongue as a "fire, full of poison, and something that no one can tame." It's a part of the body that can praise God and then turn around a curse people made in God's image. I thought about how many times I was guilty of this.

Possibly we all need to bite our tongues occasionally as a reminder to be more mindful of our blessings and to use our tongues in speech that uplifts and encourages others rather than criticizing and discouraging them.

Week 4 /Day 4

SNOWSHOES

Cast your cares on the Lord and he will sustain you; he will never let the righteous fall. Psalm 55:22

Snowshoes of various designs have been used to ease foot travel over deep snow for thousands of years. The basic idea of a snowshoe is simple: spread weight out over a larger surface area to avoid sinking deep into soft snow. Walking with snowshoes over deep snow saves energy and allows for faster travel.

Just as snowshoes keep us from sinking into deep snow, a certain level of detachment from possessions and personal power is necessary to travel a Christian path. I know in my own life I need to hold possessions more lightly and give up my illusions of control if I want to follow Jesus more closely. Worrying about and taking care of all the stuff and situations in our lives reduces our energy and freedom to do the Lord's work.

Are you sinking into responsibilities and cares that slow your pace in following the Lord? Let Him make you a pair of "no-care shoes" to stride over those worries and cares. He'll weave the webbings of grace, make the bindings of peace, and frame them in love.

Week 4 /Day 5

TRAPPER JACK

The Lord God made garments of skin for Adam and his wife and clothed them. Genesis 3:21

Late each fall a man my wife and I refer to as Trapper Jack visits the little lake by our condo to trap muskrats before it freezes over. When I talked with him, Jack indicated he had trapped up and down the west coast of Michigan for years. He had a wealth of knowledge about the plants and animals of the region and seemed to have great respect for the diversity of life around him. Still, he had no qualms about killing animals in a trap. This bothered me, but then I thought about my own meat-rich diet.

Killing animals for any reason is a serious ethical matter, one that vegetarians and vegans seek to avoid. Anyone who eats meat participates, directly or indirectly, in the killing of animals. God Himself took one of His own created beings and sacrificed it to make clothing because of His concern for Adam and Eve's welfare (Genesis 3:21). Although they had sinned, God still shared this act of love with them before they were banished from the garden.

As Christians, we should treat all creatures with reverence, awe, and a sense of holiness. Our charge of stewardship for the Earth (Genesis 2:15) was not negated when we were cast out of the Garden. Unlike in some indigenous societies dependent on hunting, the decision to eat meat or use fur and leather is a privilege many of us living in modern Western society can make. As Paul might state (1 Corinthians 6:12), killing animals for food or clothing may be permissible, but may not always be beneficial to our faith life. We must live as lightly as we can on the Earth, being thankful for all that has been provided to us.

This Coming Week

Think about the distractions in your life that slow you down in your spiritual walk. Pray for wisdom and discipline to reduce or eliminate them.

FEBRUARY DEVOTIONS

Contents:

Week 1 /Day 1

SNOWBOUND

Trust in the Lord with your whole heart and lean not on your own understanding. Proverbs 3:5

There was a blizzard in southwestern Michigan a few days before Christmas. At first just a few fine flakes started blowing through the air on the gusty, cold northeast wind. As the afternoon progressed, the snow intensified to the point that visibility was reduced to almost whiteout level. Everything seemed closed in by the intense snow, howling wind, and cold.

Our home is well built, with reliable heat and light, yet during the blizzard I felt closed in and vulnerable to the elements. I knew that it would be very difficult to go anywhere outside given the conditions and that any failure of the electricity would soon result in a very cold, dark, and uncomfortable environment.

Thinking later about my response to the blizzard conditions, I came to realize that I have a long way to go in my willingness to put my trust in the Lord. When we place our trust in our own strength (or the reliability of the electric utility company), we have placed our trust in the wrong place. This can only lead to anxiety. Trusting in the Lord, however, as the Psalms remind us, is the way to peace and joy in our lives. As it says in Psalm 37:5: "Commit your way to the Lord; trust in Him and He will do this."

The next time you feel closed in by external circumstances—whether it's a blizzard, a sickness, a loss, or whatever it may be—turn to the Lord by reading and meditating on the Psalms. There we can find peace, joy, and comfort regardless of our circumstances.

Week 1 /Day 2

OSAGE ORANGES

Jesus is the stone you builders rejected, which has become the cornerstone.
Acts 4:11

Osage orange trees, also known as "hedge apples," are native to the south-central states of Oklahoma, Texas, and Arkansas. Early settlers naturalized the tree throughout the eastern U.S and used close plantings to form fencerows for livestock.

Remnants of these fencerows can still be found in woods and fields. The large greenish-orange fruits form in the fall and litter the ground around the trees. The fruits are bitter, and usually go untouched by wildlife for most of the winter. When hunger stalks the woods in late winter, the initially rejected fruits are consumed and become lifesavers for some wildlife.

Jesus brought a lifesaving message, but those hearing Him largely rejected it. The message capsulated in the Beatitudes (Matthew 5:3-12) turned ancient Israel's world upside. The concepts of the first being last and the last first, disregard for money, total reliance on God, the Kingdom of Heaven, and losing one's life to save it still clash with the world's values.

Just as with wildlife's initial rejection of bitter Osage orange fruits, there is a bitterness for us in Jesus' message because we crave the artificial sweetness of the "good life." However, it is only when we take and eat at Jesus' banquet that we understand the lifesaving nature of living the abundant life in Him. Once we truly accept Jesus, we will wonder why we waited all winter.

Week 1 /Day 3

ICED OVER

For you died, and your life is now hidden with Christ in God. When Christ, who is in your life appears, then you also will appear with Him in glory. Colossians 3:3-4

The freshwater lake near my house in Michigan ices over each winter. The first thin ice often forms in November but usually melts as the temperatures fluctuate. Gradually, as colder days and nights become the norm, ice forms over almost the entire lake, except where the water is most exposed to the wind. Only in deepest winter will a solid layer of ice form, and all the activities associated with life on the surface of the lake—birds, amphibians, turtles, and muskrats—will cease. The body of water seemingly so alive during the summer looks like a frozen desert.

Of course, looks are deceiving, since beneath the protection of the ice life goes on. Fish still swim and forage, frogs and turtles hibernate in the mud, immature insects continue their slow development, and muskrats continue their activities in their lodges. This hidden life continues despite the bitter cold wind and snow above the layer of ice. With the return of the sun and warmth in spring, the ice will melt, the water will warm, and a seemingly new burst of life and growth will appear.

Paul explains in his letter to the Colossians that, as believers, our lives are hidden in Christ. Christ's love provides us with spiritual protection from the dangers and deceitfulness of the world the way ice protects life beneath it during the winter. Paul goes on to say in Colossians 3:4 that when Christ appears, we will also appear with Him in glory. Just as when spring returns to melt the ice, releasing a burst of new energy and growth, so Christ's return will usher in a spiritual springtime of eternal life.

Week 1 /Day 4

GLACIAL ERRATICS

They are not of the world, even as I am not of it. John 17:16

In northern portions of the Upper Midwest there are areas where glacial erratics are common. These boulder-sized chunks of volcanic granite, quartz, and other rocks were pushed south with the advancing glaciers of the last Ice Age and deposited in the glacial till left behind when the glaciers melted. These foreign geologic visitors have always fascinated me since they seem peculiar and out of place—poking out of some clay bank or laying on limestone bedrock in a stream.

Christians are called "peculiar" (1 Peter 2:9 KJV). We are not called to blend into the surrounding culture, but to be salt and light (Matthew 5:13-14). We are called to be erratic in the sense of deviating from the conventional cultural norms. As a glacial erratic is found within a geological region that it is not truly a part of, so we are called as Christians to be in the world around us but not of it (John 17:16-19). We need to continually ask ourselves whether we stand out as a voice for Christ and the Good News, or do we just blend into the landscape?

Week 1 /Day 5

DRIFTING AND LIFTING CLOUDS

Have you comprehended the vast expanses of the Earth? Tell me if you know all this. Job 38:18

Gray clouds trailing veils of light snow scudded eastward as we looked down from the 7000-foot South Rim of the Grand Canyon. A chilling wind peppered our faces with wet snowflakes as swirls of clouds not only moved overhead but also enveloped us as they lifted from the canyon below. The snowy atmosphere added a dimension of mystery, quietness, and isolation to the vastness of the canyon. In such a rarefied atmosphere, we confronted our insignificance.

As thinking beings, we constantly struggle to make God somehow in our image and likeness when, in fact, His vastness, power, and majesty, if even glimpsed, would cause us to hide ourselves in the cleft of a rock (Exodus 33:22).

It might be helpful when we pray to imagine standing at the edge of an abyss like the Grand Canyon with the power of God present and swirling around us feeling awed yet comforted by all that power and mystery. The comfort is Jesus standing by our side, holding our hand, and telling us of Abba's wild and unrelenting love for each one of us.

This Coming Week

Truly following Jesus will not always be pleasant. Jesus told James and John in Matthew 20:22 that they would need to drink the bitter cup of suffering for following him. How willing are you to suffer for Christ?

Week 2 /Day 1

ANGEL CONFETTI

Then I saw another mighty angel coming down from heaven. He was robed in a cloud with a rainbow above his head; his face was like the Sun, and his legs were like fiery pillars. Revelation 10:1

When I was a kid, our family jokingly attributed several natural phenomena to the activities of angels. Thunder was "the sound of angels bowling," rain was "angel tears," and snow was the result of "an angel pillow fight".

Angels in the Bible had more serious missions in their roles as messengers of God. A few of the many activities attributed to angels include: guarding the Garden of Eden (Genesis 3:24), speaking to Abraham (Genesis 22:11, 15), appearing to Jacob at Peniel (Genesis 28:12), destroying Sodom and Gomorrah (Genesis 19:1), leading the Israelites in the desert (Exodus 23:20), speaking to the prophets, appearing to Mary (Luke 1:28), administering to Jesus (Matthew 4:11), and giving John his revelations (Revelation 1:1).

These serious activities as messengers and agents of God make the idea of angels bowling or having a pillow fight border on the irreverent. Yet, there is no reason why angels can't relate their messages through natural phenomena.

My mother-in-law's funeral immediately comes to mind. She had struggled against cancer for several dark years before her death. Just as we were exiting the funeral home, huge snowflakes began floating down like confetti from the leaden early March skies, as if angels were celebrating the end of her suffering and welcoming her to her reward.

A childish idea—maybe. Yet, as Jesus says, unless we become like little children, we cannot enter the Kingdom of Heaven (Matthew 18:3). Angels can show themselves in many ways if we are open to them.

Week 2 /Day 2

CHANGING PERSPECTIVES

Do not be afraid or discouraged because of this vast army. For the battle is not yours, but God's. 2 Chronicles 20:15

I was always curious why the full moon often looked so large just as it came up over the eastern horizon and then appeared to shrink in size at it rose higher in the sky. The answer I found for this apparent size change is perspective.

When the moon is near the horizon, we see it compared with closer objects like trees, buildings, and hills. This makes the moon appear large. When we see the moon overhead, there is nothing nearby with which to compare it, and so it seems smaller. I still have a difficult time believing this, but obviously the moon doesn't change distance from the earth, nor is there any other reason for such an apparent size change within the matter of a few hours.

This illusion makes me think of how often I misperceive problems. Worry about some future event when it first appears often makes a problem seem much larger than it is—especially when viewed with other commitments and issues in my life. Worry is mostly a control issue. I worry about how I am going to handle the pending problem instead of how the Lord will help me handle it. Viewed from the perspective of God's role in my life, most problems eventually shrink down to manageable proportions—like a huge rising moon shrinking to its familiar size in the night sky.

Week 2 /Day 3

CLIMATE ENFORCEMENT

If any man builds on this foundation using gold, silver, costly stones, wood, hay or straw, his work will be shown for what it is, because the day will bring it to light. It will be revealed with fire, and the fire will test the quality of each man's work. 1 Corinthians 3:12-13

Bobwhite quail were common in the woods and fields of western Ohio in the late 1950s through the mid-1970s. Quail are ground-feeding birds and are very sensitive to snow and cold. Ohio is in the northern part of their range, and more than a decade of relatively mild winters allowed quail to thrive. This was followed by several very cold and snowy winters during the late 1970s. The deep snow and prolonged frigid temperatures essentially wiped out the quail populations in the northern part of their range.

Organisms thrive in areas where they are most suited to the prevailing climatic conditions. General climatic conditions are long-term (decades, centuries, or eons), while weather conditions are relatively short term (months or a few years).

Unusually mild weather conditions over several seasons will allow plants and animals not well-suited to long-term colder climatic conditions to move into areas beyond their normal range. When the weather patterns eventually change back to those more typical of the local climate, these "fair-weather species" living outside of their normal range die off.

The weather of our spiritual age and culture allows for many choices, for us to "build our houses on sand" if that is what we desire (Matthew 7:26). However, the spiritual climate God desires is one in which we love Him with all our being and honor Him in the way we live. The Bible warns repeatedly the day will come when the spiritual climate God desires will be the rule of the universe. At that point, our lives and work will be shown for what they have been (1 Corinthians 3:12), and we will know whether we are suited to live in the Kingdom's eternal climate.

Week 2 /Day 4

WHITE AS SNOW

And we, who with unveiled faces all reflect the Lord's glory, are being transformed into His likeness with ever-increasing glory, which comes from the Lord, who is Spirit. 2 Corinthians 3:18

Although fresh-fallen snow appears to cover everything with a pure white blanket, it holds every color of the rainbow and more. A snowy scene only appears to be white because all the jumbled snow crystals and air pockets scatter light in all directions. This reflects to our eyes as white—the color of pure sunlight.

The brilliance and light of God is depicted several times in the Bible as being white as snow (Daniel 7:9; Matthew 28:3; Revelation 1:14). Paul compares the need for Moses to veil his face on Mount Sinai in the presence of God's brilliance to our ability through Jesus to experience God's presence unveiled.

In 2 Corinthians 3, Paul goes on to state that we, with unveiled faces, all reflect God's glory. We are being transformed into His likeness with ever increasing glory that comes from a life in the Spirit. Just as snow reflects the pure essence of white sunlight, in the Spirit of the Lord, we can reflect the pure essence of the Son.

Week 2 /Day 5

GRAVITY

He himself is before all things, and in Him all things hold together.
Colossians 1:17 NRSV

Gravity holds our earthly world and the entire solar system together.
The tremendous mass of the Earth creates a pull on everything
around it—including the oceans, the moon, you and me. Without
Earth's gravity, we would literally float away into the universe. Even
the air we breathe would vanish into space. Without the gravity of
the moon pulling on the Earth, we wouldn't have ocean tides and
Earth would wobble, and without the gravity of the sun, Earth itself
would fly off into space.

God is the most tremendous spiritual and physical force in the
universe. His love pulls on our souls and keeps us grounded in faith.
Paul states that Jesus has always existed with the Father and the
Holy Spirit and that He holds all things together. This means God is
involved in every physical aspect of the universe as we know it, from
subatomic and atomic particles to giant stars and black holes.
Most importantly, God's love continues to pull us to Him, and, just
as with gravity, there is nothing we can really do about it. We can
allow sin in our lives to spin us off into selfishness, but no matter
what, there always remains a pull of God's love.

This Coming Week

Change is constant in the natural world. Pay attention this week to
subtle transformations around you—an opening flower bud, a
changing leaf, weather changes or other natural phenomena.

Week 3 /Day 1

ONLY GOD CAN MAKE A TREE

He bore our sins in his body on the tree, that we might die to sin and live to righteousness. By His wounds you have been healed. 1Peter 2:24 ESV

God's omnipotence and total knowledge of the physical world are incomprehensible. While walking through the woods, I've sometimes thought about His all-encompassing knowledge of every cell, molecule, and atom of every living thing. He is aware of and intimately knows the flow of water and sap up and down the trunks of the trees, the photosynthesis going on within each green leaf, the moisture being absorbed by each tiny root hair. Each tree is truly a miracle.

Consider the tree that was cut down to make the cross for our Savior. Although God knew the eventual use of this tree, He blessed it with the growing conditions that allowed it to grow to the size for its final use. Jesus entered His creation and humbled Himself to be crucified by the people, tools, and the cross itself, which, although perverted in purpose by sin, were still lovingly sustained by Him. .

As the tree for the cross grew, it was blessed; and as the nails were driven, we were blessed. It impossible to comprehend the vastness of God's love just as it is impossible to comprehend the vastness of His knowledge, but through a life of faith, we can accept both with gratefulness and awe.

Week 3 /Day 2

ASHES TO LIFE

I baptize you with water for repentance. But after me will come one who is more powerful than I, whose sandals I am not fit to carry. He will baptize you with the Holy Spirit and with fire. Matthew 3:11

My wife and I went to an Ash Wednesday service where a cross of ashes was placed on our foreheads. This was done to remind us of our mortality and of God's love and mercy through Jesus. The Catholic Church burns palm fronds to make the ashes, but the use of burned pine needles would be just as appropriate.

Pitch Pine, Table Mountain Pine, Jack Pine, Longleaf Pine, and other pine species are dependent upon periodic fires to open their cones and release seeds. The cones of these pines are sealed with resin, which must be melted to open and release seeds for a new generation of trees. Fire also releases nutrients in the needles and duff beneath the trees, which will benefit any new seedlings. New life for these pines only can come from fire and ashes. Without fire, these species would perish.

The ashes of Ash Wednesday remind us of the spiritual regenerative power of Lenten observances such as prayer and fasting. Lent is a time to remember that we are of unclean lips that can be cleansed by the burning embers of the Spirit (Isaiah 6:7). Only when we also are crucified with Christ (Galatians 2:20) can our lives effectively spread the Good News all around us, just as a fire-opened pinecone spreads its seeds.

Week 3 /Day 3

MIXED SIGNALS

Therefore, rid yourselves of all malice and all deceit, hypocrisy,
envy, and slander of every kind. 1 Peter 2:1

As I was walking down a suburban street in Phoenix, Arizona, one
January afternoon, I noticed something unusual about the street
trees. The ornamental crabapples had white blossoms bursting open,
while at the same time their yellowing leaves were dropping to the
ground. The trees were responding to mixed seasonal cues. The
daylight hours were short and winter-like, while the temperatures
were moderate and spring-like. The trees were obviously "confused"
by these mixed signals.

As Christians we often send mixed signals to the world around us.
We say we believe in the Bible but may never have read it. We say we
follow Christ's teachings of love and forgiveness, but our lives reveal
hate and anger and grudges. We say that we love our Creator, but we
abuse the creation as much or more than any nonbeliever. Unless
our actions line up with our stated beliefs, we send mixed signals to
everyone around us.

We need to distinguish between honest failings and hypocritical
living. No Christian has fully lived a Christ-life since, we are all, and
will continue to be sinners. Sadly, the diametrically opposed words
and actions of many Christians have likely turned more seekers away
from a faith in Christ than just about anything else. As Emerson said,
"Your actions speak so loudly, I cannot hear what you say."

The way to avoid being hypocrites is to fully recognize our sinfulness
and to repent daily for our individual and corporate shortcomings
(1 Corinthians 10:12-13). An honest assessment and admission of our
failings as Christians will not only keep us from sending mixed
signals but will allow the grace and love of Christ to grow within us
(1 John 5:4-5).

Week 3 /Day 4

LONG PREPARATION TIMES

After forty years had passed, an angel appeared to Moses in the flames of a burning bush in the desert near Mount Sinai. Acts 7:30

In observing God's creation, I've noticed in many instances how the length of time spent in developing is long compared to the length of time spent in maturity or adulthood. Leaf buds on some deciduous trees form in mid-summer but don't open until the following spring. Many insects spend the greater part of their lives in immature stages of development having adult life spans that may cover only a few days, during which they find mates, lay eggs, and die.

Preparation times for many of the leaders and prophets in the Bible were also quite long. Think of Moses tending Jethro's sheep for 40 years, Joshua spending over 80 years in the desert with Moses and the Israelites, and Jesus, who spent many years preparing prior to beginning His public ministry.

In our Christian walk, we often get impatient with God during our preparation times. We want to get moving, we don't understand why our ministry is not going well, or why it seems like we pray for something for so long and nothing seems to happen. It's times like these that we need to understand God's timing.

A spiritual life is a life of preparation and growth, of future maturity. We must accept that sometimes we may never see the fruits of our preparations on Earth, but that doesn't mean our faithful actions during preparation times won't be fruitful, won't impact others. As Paul said, some are called to plant, some to water, and others to harvest (1 Corinthians 3:4-8).

Week 3 /Day 5

SNOW-CAPPED ROCKS

Then the angel showed me the river of the water of life as clear as crystal flowing from the throne of God and of the Lamb. Revelation 22:1

As I was walking along a small stream near our house last winter, the waters glistened in the morning sun. A winter night of quiet, wet snowfall had transformed each emergent rock into miniature snow-capped peaks. The visual beauty of the scene was enhanced by the intricate tones of burbling water softly rising into the still cold air.

Just as the stream waters swirling around the snow-capped rocks are always new and ever changing, so it is with God's grace in our lives, providing new mercies every day (Lamentations 3:23). Even in the worst of times, in times of loss and grieving, the river of God surrounds us with comfort and "bestows upon us a crown of beauty instead of ashes, the oil of gladness instead of mourning, and a garment of praise instead of a spirit of despair" (Isaiah 61:3).

Let's allow the Lord's beauty to cover us as snow-capped rocks immersed in His continuous stream of love. As the lyrics of the hymn "All is Well with My Soul" aptly state, we can have "peace like a river" if we stay in the flow of God's love and grace.

This Coming Week

Read the lyrics of "All is Well with My Soul."

Week 4 /Day 1

GOD OF FIRE

I have come to bring fire on the earth, and how I wish it were already kindled! Luke 12:49

Fire is essential to human life, as we know it. We've learned to control fire to warm our homes, power our vehicles, turn electrical turbines, and to generally keep human industry running. All fire we use on Earth originates from energy originally released from the sun. The sun is a magnificent creation of God, but when we look to the heavens on a clear night, we can see thousands of distant stars many much larger than the sun. Our Creator God has set the universe on fire.

The Bible refers to fire in many ways. There is the pillar of fire leading the Israelites through the desert night (Exodus 13:21), the sacrificial fires in Leviticus, punishing fires and purifying fires throughout the Bible, and the fire of the Holy Spirit (Acts 2:3). God himself is even referred to as a "consuming fire" (Exodus 24:17; Deuteronomy 9:3; Hebrews 12:29).

By its nature, fire is transformative and powerful. The message of Jesus is also transformative and powerful to those who are open to it. It is the fire of the Holy Spirit that purifies and enlightens us to God's working in both the physical and spiritual realms surrounding us. We are transformed into the children of God we were created to be. Our prayer should be that an unquenchable fire of love for our God never ceases.

Week 4 /Day 2

THE SUN IN GRANDPA'S EYES

What does man gain from all the toil at which he toils under the sun? A generation comes and a generation goes, but the earth remains forever. The sun rises and the sun goes down and hastens to the place where it rises. Ecclesiastes 1:3-5 ESV

I like to pay attention to the way sunlight strikes people in old family photos. It's interesting to look at the shadows on their faces as well as the shadows their figures cast on the surroundings. The subjects are often squinting as they look into the camera. It strikes me how I'm living my own life beneath the same sun that illuminated my ancestors on that day long ago.

A general theme mentioned many times in the Book of Ecclesiastes is that we are born out of darkness, and we live our physical lives only briefly in the sunlight before returning to the darkness of the grave. The sun continues after us, just as it had shone before us—shining on the good and the bad with indifference.

However, before getting too depressed about the brevity of earthly life under the sun, I try to keep in mind that I am a spiritual being on a journey within an eternal life. We are heading to where the 'Son' shines all the time, with nothing but healing and love.

Week 4 /Day 3

REFLECTION ON A REFLECTION

It will be established forever like the moon, a faithful witness in the sky. Psalm 89:37

What is it about the moon that so fascinates us? Maybe being creatures of the day (Psalm 104:23), we humans long for light during the night. Or it may be because the moon changes its appearance in the sky as it cycles between full and new. Even ancient peoples reverenced the moon and its association with the natural cycles of growth, reproduction, and tidal changes. Periodic lunar eclipses were also times of fear since their cause was not understood.

Even though we may consider ourselves much more sophisticated in our understanding of the moon, there is still something about God's lesser light (Genesis 1:14) that captures our imaginations. The glow of a rising full moon over the horizon, the softness of moonlight on a snowy field, or a child's imaginings of the Man in the Moon provide comforting and peaceful thoughts regardless of how much astronomy we might know.

As a reflection of the sun, the moon reminds us that the sun is still shining even when we are on the dark side of the planet. It's an assurance that another sunrise is coming, another day. As Christians, we are "lesser lights" of the Son. Our calling is to reflect the Good News into the darkness of the world around us.

Week 4 /Day 4

SURROUNDED AND IMMERSED

The wind blows wherever it pleases. You hear its sound, but you cannot tell where it comes from or where it is going. So it is with everyone born of the Spirit. John. 3:8

I love the praise song "Breathe." The lyrics state that, like the air we breathe, God's holy presence lives in us. God not only surrounds us with His presence, but also penetrates through our entire physical and spiritual being. Many New Testament scripture passages compare the Holy Spirit to the earth's breath (wind) and reference both the life-giving and purifying nature of it, along with water (John 3:8; John 3:5; Romans. 6:4; Ephesians 5:26).

Both air and water, which are critical to life, continually move around, into, and out of all the earth's living and non-living systems. Water is constantly evaporating from water bodies, soil, plants and even us before returning through condensation and precipitation. Air molecules not only continually circle the globe but also are removed and replaced by plants through photosynthesis. Many of the air molecules we breathe today are the same as those breathed by Jesus during His life on Earth.

The first look at Earth from space sent back by the Apollo astronauts in 1968 was a perspective-changing event for much of humankind. We saw more clearly than ever before the beauty of our blue and white planet, and we saw how utterly unique and alone we are in the vastness of space. Over the subsequent years, we have become more aware of the interconnectedness of all life on Earth and of the beautiful way the Lord designed the earth to support life. How often do we stop to think about the miracle of God's love, surrounding us in the very air we breathe and the water we drink? You don't have to go far to experience a miracle. Just take a deep breath.

Week 4 /Day 5

FIELD MARKS

By their fruit you will recognize them. Matthew 7:16

Wing bars, eye rings, bill length, and throat patch—all are field mark terms used to describe the bird in the brush or across the lake or soaring above. Serious birders will spend hours studying photographs and drawings of various species. They will also go bird watching frequently to hone their skills at recognizing species on the wing.

As Christians, what are our field marks? Physical appearances certainly are not reliable for identification. We come in all colors, shapes, and sizes, wear many different styles of clothing, and live in every imaginable habitat. Simply doing good works in the community and living moral and ethical lives are also not definitive. Ethical living can be done by anyone, regardless of what they do or do not believe. Great amounts of money can be given to charity not so much for the good it does for the poor, but with the motivation of the giver to be recognized and remembered as a philanthropist. Donations of time and money may not be altruistic but rather may come from a feeling of superiority or pity.

So what is the best Christian field mark? It's *agape* (a word derived from Greek meaning "unconditional love"). Agape love does not desire or expect any reward or recognition. It is also given knowing it may be rejected. It reflects the love Jesus shows to us. Unconditional love given in the name of Jesus—it's the distinguishing field mark of a true Christian.

This Coming Week

"We can do no great things, only small things with great love," said Mother Theresa. Be thankful for all small things you can do in His name here on God's beautiful garden we call Earth.

MARCH DEVOTIONS

Contents:

Week 1 /Day 1

SPRING SNOWSTORM IN THE SMOKIES

From Zion perfect in beauty, God shines forth. Psalm 50:2

My wife and I were returning home to Ohio from a late March meeting in South Carolina. We had planned to take the Newfound Gap Road through Great Smoky Mountain National Park, but an early spring snowstorm changed our plans. We ended up taking the long way around the park to reach our overnight destination of Gatlinburg, Tennessee.

The day following the storm dawned bright with a deep blue sky. As we looked up into the mountains, we were dazzled by the glittering brilliance of ice-coated trees. Although we hadn't planned it, we decided to take time to drive up into the wonderland of ice and snow. At the lower elevations, every intricate ice-coated needle and branch sparkled in the brilliant sunlight. Crystals seemed to fall from the sky as the Sun's warmth increased, melting the ice sculptures. We felt as if we were moving through pure beauty and breathing it in.

Physical beauty can be found in many places, but there is a deeper, purer beauty permeating the universe. What we admire using our senses is only a poor representation of God's glorious beauty. We see through a glass, darkly (1 Corinthians 13:12). Yet the Good News continues to break through where love prevails. It is the beauty of this love of Christ that will, as Dostoevsky states, save the world.

Week 1 /Day 2

NO HURRY

Woe . . . to those who say, "Let God hurry; let Him hasten His work so we may see it. The plan of the Holy One of Israel—let it approach, let it come into view, so we may know it." Isaiah 5:18-19

Our culture of work and consumerism doesn't look kindly on true relaxation or slow steady progress. Consider the expression "as exciting as watching grass grow." If actions are to be believed, this is not a favorite pastime of most folks. We are people in a hurry—a hurry to get to work, a hurry to finish work, a hurry to make money, a hurry to go have fun, and maybe even in a hurry to make a difference for God.

Hurrying is often accompanied by anxiety that takes our attention away from the preciousness of each moment. Our headlong rush to get to the next thing steals our sense of wonder at God's created world and our care for each other and the creation. The faster our world seems to move, the less time we have to question why it needs to move so fast.

This all-consuming need for speed is not something generally seen in God's creation. Instead, we observe timely and measured processes. Plant growth, flowering, seed production, animal migrations and breeding times (in response to seasonal changes) give testimony to a Creator who works efficiently and yet without hurry.

In Scripture, we don't see Jesus hurrying even when His friend Lazarus was dying (John 11:6). Even when His earthly end was at hand, Jesus took the time to have a meal with His disciples (Matthew 26:20).

As Christians, let us take a lesson from both the life of Jesus and from His creation. Slow down to look, listen, and to show our love for each other and for all God has created in His time. We are eternal beings. Take it from the Lord, there's really no reason to hurry.

Week 1 /Day 3

HOUSEGUESTS

I pray that out of his glorious riches He may strengthen you with power through his Spirit in your inner being. Ephesians 3:16

Houseguests reside in every cell of our bodies. These guests are called mitochondria, and we couldn't live without them since they are responsible for converting nutrients and oxygen in cells into energy. They are guests from the standpoint that they divide and multiply independently of the cells themselves. We literally could not breathe without these mitochondrial powerhouses that we only inherit from our mothers.

Just as a cell cannot survive without mitochondria, souls cannot survive without the Holy Spirit. The Spirit empowers us to live our lives for Christ. Jesus received this power when John baptized Him in the Jordan, and He proclaimed this power through the Spirit at the beginning of His ministry (Luke 4:18).

Let us thank the Lord each day for the gift of physical life made possible by our mitochondrial houseguests and, more importantly, for the gift of a life in Christ through the indwelling spiritual power of the Holy Spirit (Ephesians 3:16).

Week 1 /Day 4

BEAUTY IN IMPERFECTION

Be perfect, therefore, as your heavenly Father is perfect. Matthew 5:48

I have a photograph near my desk of a weathered and twisted cedar tree pointing its gnarled finger-like branch to the sky. It's certainly not the loveliest cedar tree, but its imperfection is what makes it so appealing. There are similar examples of beautiful imperfections everywhere—a wooden bowl made from a damaged chunk of maple burl, an old piece of china with cracked glaze, an old torn and worn pair of jeans—none perfect, but all perfectly wonderful.

Although Christ calls His followers to be *in* the world and not *of* the world (John 17:14), it is almost impossible for us to not be affected by the demands of our culture. The media constantly bombards us with what how we are supposed to live—our culture's idea of beauty, success, and happiness. The demands are so prevalent that it's easy to become ensnared in this false value system. In the quest to reach the unreachable, it's possible to harm ourselves, to hurt one another, and to damage the Earth. As Matthew states, "What good will it be for someone to gain the whole world, yet forfeit their soul?" (Matthew 16:26)

The fact is, nothing in this world is perfect—not you, not me, not anything. Yet everything is unique in its imperfection. As followers of Christ, we are only called to perfection in love, which we realize will never totally be attained in this life. God loves us, warts and all. Our call is to love God back and to love each other as God loves us, even if our love is imperfect.

Week 1 /Day 5

DOVES OF PROMISE

See! The winter is past; the rains are over and gone. Flowers appear on the earth; the season of singing has come, the cooing of doves is heard in our land. Song of Songs 4:11-12

In the Upper Midwest, the winters can seem to drag on from one cold dark day to another. Despite the typical weather of a late January or early February day, I always look forward to hearing the first cooing of Mourning Doves. Despite the still-frigid temperatures, the doves will consistently respond to the slightest lengthening of daylight by breaking their winter silence. Thus, the doves are not "mourning," as their common name would suggest, but are singing a new song of the promise of spring.

Throughout the Bible, doves are symbols of promise. Noah sent out doves to find dry land (Genesis 8:8). Mary and Joseph offered doves at Jesus's purification in the temple (Luke 2:24), and the Holy Spirit descended as a dove at Jesus's baptism by John, signaling the beginning of His ministry (Matthew 3:16).

We all experience our own winters—times of sadness, sickness, and suffering. However, even during these dark times, we need to continually listen and look for that promise of the peace of Christ breaking through into our lives. The Mourning Dove's song is heard as winter comes to an end. The promise and hope of Jesus's love can be experienced during our own personal winter when we hear His words through Scripture, from other brothers and sisters in Christ, and from spending time in His creation.

This Coming Week

At what time in your life's winters have you experienced the promise and hope of Jesus's love?

Week 2 /Day 1

LAKE OR POND?

Then Jesus asked, "What is the Kingdom of God like? What shall I compare it to? It is like a mustard seed, which a man took and planted in his garden. It grew and became a tree and the birds of the air perched in its branches." Luke. 13:18-19

While lakes have names on maps, most ponds are nameless, at least beyond their immediate locality. I'm not sure when a body of water is big enough or important enough to be named a lake.

Although lakes may gain more attention from mapmakers, modest little ponds are often more important to the people and the environment in their immediate vicinity. I think of all the borrow pit ponds along interstate highways where soil was excavated to construct overpasses. Many of these ponds have been developed for fishing, swimming, boating, camping, and other recreational activities, which serve the surrounding community. What comes most to mind are the ponds of my youth where summer days were spent fishing for bluegills and winter afternoons were spent ice-skating.

Spiritually, I think most of us Christians are ponds. Our names do not appear on the maps that show famous religious figures, great evangelists, or missionaries. Instead, we live quiet lives, interacting mostly with family, friends, and acquaintances. But like the ponds that local people cherish as swimming holes, fishing places, or just as places of quiet beauty, we often touch lives that surround us in ways more meaningful than can some distant religious figure.

In the Kingdom of Heaven, little things mean a lot. Tiny mustard seeds of love sown by us can grow into trees spreading their branches into the surroundings, providing sustenance and shelter for all in Christ's name. Little nameless ponds provide beauty and joy to those nearby. Let's be content to be ponds filled with the Living Waters of Christ, becoming a blessing to anyone in the neighborhood.

Week 2 /Day 2

CAPSTONES

"The stone the builders rejected has become the capstone." Psalm 118:22.

My wife and I took an afternoon walk along the beach the day after an early spring windstorm had blown in across Lake Michigan. The storm left the beach area covered with gravel-size stones, which were large enough to remain in place despite the ferocious wind.

We noticed that there were several areas where small little sculpted towers of finer sand had been formed by the wind. Each of these sand towers had caps of more wind-resistant sand or gravel on top of them. These little sand formations reminded me of miniature versions of hoodoos and buttes in the West. Both hoodoos and buttes were formed when more erosion-resistant capstones protected the rock beneath them. As a result, the protected rock and soil withstood the wind and water that washed away the surrounding unprotected rock.

As Christians, we need to have Jesus as our capstone of protection. Without Him, we are prone to being blown to the four winds or washed away in the floodwaters of life. It's only when we place our relationship with Jesus as the top priority in our life that we find protection under the shadow of His wings (Psalm 91:1). If our relationship with Jesus has a lower priority in our lives, all that has a higher priority is at great risk of being eroded away.

Week 2 /Day 3

EARLY SPRING WOODLAND PASTELS

He told them this parable: "Look at the fig tree and all trees. When they sprout leaves, you can see for yourselves and know that summer is near. Even so, when you see these things happening, you know that the kingdom of God is near." Luke 21:29-30

Fall is time of beautiful tree colors in the Northeast and Midwest. However, in early spring, at bud-break, there is another beautiful (often understated) pallet of pastels painted by the deciduous woodland trees. The soft early spring sunlight brings out a magnificent blending of pale yellows, reds, and greens, as in a pointillist painting. The same bold autumn colors seen in a tree's leaves are apparent in a much-subdued way for a few days. Unlike the autumn splashes of leaf colors noticed by practically everyone, subtle spring woodland colors often go unnoticed.

In a way, Jesus's earthly ministry was a spiritual bud-break. His life on Earth was the beginning of a long-awaited "springtime," though many missed the subtlety of the Carpenter from Nazareth. They were looking for the immediate blazing colors of an earthly messianic king, and, for that reason, many today still dismiss Jesus's message.

The dominant colors of Jesus's message are love, reconciliation, and forgiveness. Sometimes we find these colors difficult to see in the world around us and even in ourselves, but if we truly believe in Jesus, they become visible, seen with eyes of faith. When He returns in "blazing color," many will wonder how they missed that subtle springtime "bud-break".

Week 2 /Day 4

BIRTH OF SPRING

By the tender mercy of our God, the dawn from on high will break upon us, to give light to those who sit in darkness and in the shadow of death, to guide our feet into the way of peace. Luke 1:78-79 NRSV

A winter in southern Arizona is barely winter. Low temperatures rarely dip below freezing, and sunny afternoon highs are usually at least in the 60s. Shrubs and flowers begin blooming in mid-February. Birds begin singing and establishing mates and territories about the same time.

It is in Southern Arizona, along with south Texas and Florida, where spring for the United States is birthed and begins its inexorable march northward, advancing at sea level approximately 17 miles—and in altitude 100 feet—per day.

In the Upper Midwest, year-round resident birds such as Mourning Doves and House Finches are the prophets of spring. They begin their springtime cooing and singing in February, well in advance of spring warmth. Snowdrifts may still be piled high, but the birds aren't chirping about the weather. Instead, their spring songs begin as they respond to the lengthening daylight. It's not about the weather. It's all about the sun.

For Christians, spring is all about the Son in our lives, too—His resurrection. We too sing our praises, regardless of surrounding circumstances (1 Thessalonians 5:18). When we keep our minds focused on the Lord and His mercy and grace, we remain in springtime peace, even though still surrounded by the unsettling cold of winter (Isaiah 26:3).

Week 2 /Day 5

EARTH SHADOW

May my prayer be set before you like incense; may the lifting up of my hands be like the evening sacrifice. Psalm 141:2

As a beautiful desert sunset blazed across the western sky, I turned and looked to the east. There, along the horizon, the sky was a blackish purple. It was the rising shadow of the Earth cast out into space away from the sun.

Being creatures of the day, we have a deep-seated fear of darkness and night, yet God has used and continues to use nighttime as an integral feature of His creation. Night ushers in a time of rest and an opportunity for prayer and connecting with the Lord. Nighttime is when God speaks in dreams (Isaac, Samuel, Daniel), when signs and wonders have occurred, from manna appearing daily for the Israelites to the worship of the infant Jesus by the shepherds.

The coming of night is a daily reminder that all of creation is made to work in cycles of activity and rest. In our culturally driven strivings for more and more and never-ending activity, we sometimes neglect the rest we need for ourselves and the rest that is needed by all of creation on a daily and seasonal basis. Pushing ourselves and the creation beyond God's set limits leads to physical and spiritual damage. As stated in Ecclesiastes, there is a time for everything— including rest for body and soul in Earth's shadow.

This Coming Week

Participate in Jesus's "bud-break" of the Kingdom of God by showing small acts of kindness and thankfulness in whatever situations you encounter—maybe a note to a friend, an extra tip to a waiter or waitress, a payment for someone standing in a grocery line with only a couple of items. Be creative!

Week 3 /Day 1

HALOS AND HOLINESS

For it is written, "You shall be holy, for I am holy." 1 Peter 1:13-16 NRSV

As I looked out across the Sonoran Desert landscape one sunny winter afternoon, it appeared as though all the spiny cholla cacti were outlined by whitish halos. A similar phenomenon can be observed with the heads of teasel, thistles, cattails, and any other plant or plant part having many fine spines or fuzzy seed heads illuminated from behind by the sun.

Although halos are not mentioned in the Bible, Middle Age and Renaissance painters often depicted Christ, the apostles, saints, and others with their heads surrounded by a halo. A halo was used to denote holiness.

One definition of *holy* is "to be set apart for the service and worship of God". The Bible calls us to be holy as God is holy (1 Peter 1:13-16; Leviticus 11:14, 19:2, 20:7). We pursue holiness through the process of sanctification under the guidance of the Holy Spirit. It's a lifetime of work for the believer.

What about the rest of creation, including those spiny cholla cacti? Are they holy? I believe they are. God declared His creation as "good". No part of creation (other than humankind) has any choice but to exist in its own mysterious way for the service and worship of God. No matter where we are, we are surrounded by the holiness of creation. However, God leaves it up to us to decide whether we are also clothed in holiness.

Week 3 /Day 2

WATER-WORN ROCKS

If your brother or sister sins, go and point out their fault, just between the two of you. If they listen to you, you have won them over. But if they will not listen, take one or two others along, so that every matter may be established by the testimony of two or three witnesses. Matthew 18:15-16

I have three basaltic rocks on my desk. One I picked up along the Washington coast, and the other two along the shoreline of Lake Superior. Two are gray and one is black, but they all had a similar volcanic origin. They were broken loose from larger pieces of rock and spent years of being rubbed and polished against other rocks and sand by the movement of waves and water. When I look at these stones, I think of the praise song, "Waves of Mercy (Every Move I Make)." The first line of the chorus is: "Waves of mercy, waves of grace."

We start our lives as very self-centered beings, but as we age, through our interactions with our environment and community, we are polished into more thoughtful adults. Often many rough edges of self-centeredness remain even though we mature physically. Belonging to a Christian community where we hold each other accountable (Matthew 18:15-18) helps with smoothing the rough edges. We need the Lord, and we need each other to truly become a well-worn piece of the Rock that shows what His waves of mercy and waves of grace can do.

Week 3 /Day 3

PRAISES IN THE AIR

Do not let any unwholesome talk come out of your mouths, but only what is helpful for building others up according to their needs, that it may benefit those who listen. Ephesians 4:29

Although there is reference to sky in Genesis, the Bible does not speak directly about the creation of the air/atmosphere. Yet we know that without air, life as God created it could not exist. Sound also cannot exist without air. Praise music, prayer, hymns, and other verbal expressions of praise would be impossible, if it were not for air.

Every singing bird, chirping cricket, and howling wolf is praising God in its own way. Even the inanimate world gives voice to God's having breathed life into the world. Consider the sounds of crashing waves, rumbling volcanoes, calving glaciers, whispering wind through the trees, and howling hurricane winds. These are all part of God's creation. We can only experience the sounds associated with all these because of air.

The air surrounding us sustains our physical life and allows us, along with all of creation, to sing out our praises (Psalm 66:4). As we breathe in life-giving air, let us strive to breathe out sounds of gratitude and praise.

Week 3 /Day 4

CROWS

The ravens brought him bread and meat in the morning and bread and meat in the evening, and he drank from the brook. 1 Kings 17:6

Crows and ravens both belong to the bird family Corvidae. Corvids are social birds rarely found alone. In studies conducted by ornithologists, crows and ravens have been found to form family units and to even care for each other's offspring. They often warn of the presence of hawks or owls by loudly cawing, and they will mob (aerially attack) a hawk or even an eagle on the wing. Of course, crows and ravens also have their not-so-noble traits, like stealing other birds' eggs and killing the young of other bird species, but Biblically crows—and their raven cousins—are found to be honorable.

God certainly picked one of the smartest of His birds to sustain Elijah. (Although, as notorious scavengers, I wonder what kinds of food the ravens provided!) Noah also picked a raven to send out of the ark before sending out a dove to look for dry land (Genesis 8:7). Several Bible passages refer to God caring for the raven (Job 38:41; Psalm 147:9) Jesus also referred to the ravens of the air and how God takes care of their needs (Luke 12:24).

Like ravens and crows, humans are for the most part intelligent, familial, and honorable, and, like these birds, God cares for us. In fact, referring to ravens, Jesus mentions how much more valuable we are to God than these wonderful birds He created. So, the next time you hear a crow or raven call, remember God loves you and that you are valuable to Him no matter what not-so-noble traits you may have. Just let Him work in your life. If the Lord can use birds, He can certainly use you!

Week 3 /Day 5

DRESSED FOR THE OCCASION

Rather, clothe yourselves with the Lord Jesus Christ, and do not think about how to gratify the desires of the flesh. Romans 13:14

Goldfinches are often a source of confusion among novice bird watchers. New birders have trouble distinguishing between the olive-drab female and the male goldfinch's dull, brown plumage of winter, which turns bright lemony yellow each spring. Of course, many bird species undergo similar seasonal changes in color and patterning. Brighter colors and stronger patterns are important for males to successfully find a mate, while females of the same species are often less colorful, to blend in better with vegetation surrounding nest sites. God's plan for these creatures ensures that they are properly dressed for all the occasions of their lives.

In the Christian walk, we are properly dressed spiritually only when we clothe ourselves in the righteousness of Christ. If we try to be righteous on our own, we become like the man in the parable of the wedding feast (Matthew 22:11-14) who the king found to be improperly attired. The man refused to put on the wedding garments that were customarily provided to all guests by the host. He was thrown out of the wedding feast because he was not dressed for the occasion.

When we clothe ourselves in Christ, we will always be properly dressed for any occasion, including meeting our King face to face.

This Coming Week

Look through your closet. If you have articles of clothing that are in good condition, but that you haven't worn for months or years, consider donating them to a charity.

Week 4 /Day 1

COMPANION PLANTING

For where two or three gather in my name, there am I with them.
Matthew 18:20

Many gardeners use a technique called "companion planting" to
increase their garden's productivity. The technique involves planting
certain flowers and vegetables near each other for mutual benefit. A
good example is the "Three Sisters" (corn, pole beans, and squash)
method that was widely practiced by many Native American tribes.
In this case, the pole beans would climb on the corn stalks and (as a
legume) also restore nitrogen to the soil, which fertilized both the
corn and squash. The squash shaded the soil reducing moisture loss
and limiting weed growth.

The need for mutual support in the Christian faith walk was evident
from the beginnings of the Church (Acts 2:42-47). These early
Christians supported each other in their faith growth and in their
physical and social needs.

The chances are that whatever church you may be attending or just
visiting has some type of small group ministry. This concept runs
counter to much of our culture's individualistic and online-only
approach to social interaction. Well-run small groups offer a chance
to widen our horizons of social relationships, grow in our
understanding of our faith, and join with others in prayer.

If you don't belong to a small group within your church, consider
joining one or starting one yourself.

Week 4 /Day 2

EMBRACING RAINY DAYS

He covers the sky with clouds; He supplies the earth with rain and makes grass grow on the hills. Psalm 147:8

For creatures being composed of 90 percent water and requiring fresh drinking water daily, we don't seem to have much appreciation for rain. Many of us grumble about rainy weather, how it ruins outdoor plans, whether those are picnics, parades, or sporting events. We want sunshine all the time.

City-based TV weather forecasters praise sunny warm days even when the corn crop is wilting. It's only when true drought takes hold—drying up water reservoirs or increasing the hazards of wildfires—do people start hoping and praying for clouds and rain. Water is a key to life on Earth, and the wonderful water cycle of evaporation, condensation, and precipitation is truly a gift from God.

As Psalm 118:24 says, "This is the day the Lord has made, let us rejoice and be glad in it!" Even a rainy day is a special gift that not only brings life-sustaining water to the Earth, but also can draw people together inside for shelter.

A rainy day can encourage us to slow down and enjoy a good book or to pursue some other indoor activity. Instead of grumbling next time it rains on your parade, thank God for His provision of water and spend some time praying and reading Scripture, enjoying the company of Jesus, the source of living water.

Week 4 /Day 3

GOLD IN THE HILLS

These [trials] have come so that your faith—of greater worth than gold, which perishes even though refined by fire—may be proved genuine and may result in praise, glory and honor when Jesus Christ is revealed. 1 Peter 1:7

During the late 1800s, gold prospectors scoured the Superstition Mountains of Arizona in search of gold. Rumors of finding the mother lode abounded among the prospectors, driving them on to want to strike it rich. Although some gold was found and a few mines operated for a time in the area, great fortunes were never made.

Nevertheless, several times a decade, gold can be found in abundance in the Superstitions. This isn't the metallic variety, but rather Mexican gold poppies. When the autumn and winter rains have fallen at the right time and in the right amounts, the spring desert blooms with wildflowers, including blankets of Mexican gold poppies, which cover the mountainsides.

Jesus referred to the splendor of wildflowers when He spoke of the lilies of the field (Matthew 6:28 and Luke 12:27). These passages of Scripture are part of Jesus's admonition against worrying and chasing after riches rather than seeking the Kingdom and storing up eternal treasure in heaven. In your consideration of what's worth pursuing in your life, which gold are you feverish for—the one of riches, like the prospectors in the Superstition Mountains sought (in vain), or the gold wildflower "fever" of the Holy Spirit?

Week 4 /Day 4

VERNAL POOLS

Let us acknowledge the Lord; let us press on to acknowledge Him. As surely as the Sun rises, He will appear; He will come to us like the winter rains, like the spring rains that water the earth. Hosea 6:3

As a kid growing up in rural western Ohio, I would often ride my bike out to explore a small woodlot not too far from our house. Although there were no ponds in the woodlot, there were several shallow pools that formed every spring. The water in these pools teemed with tiny crustaceans called fairy shrimp, but as summer approached, the pools would shrink in size and finally dry up. I didn't know it at the time, but ecologists call these temporary ponds "vernal pools" (*vernal* referring to springtime).

Vernal pools are important for many creatures—particularly frogs and salamanders that breed in these temporary habitats and whose young feed on fairy shrimp and other tiny organisms. Timing is critical to the breeding success of these amphibians, since mating and complete development must be accomplished in a short period (between early spring warming and disappearance of the pools in late spring). The life cycles of amphibians using these pools are fine-tuned to God's timing of the seasons.

I sometimes think how out of synch with God's timing my life is. I like to think I can forge my own way, make my own plans, but often I'm thwarted by one kind of problem or another. Being somewhat of a control freak, waiting on the Lord is not one of my strong points. It's at those points in my life that I need to think more in terms of vernal-pool timing. God is always on time. My job is to fine-tune my life to that fact.

Week 4 /Day 5

DAYS TO MATURITY

Teach us to number our days aright, that we may gain a heart of wisdom. Psalm 90:12

Seed packets contain a lot of vital information for the gardener. One of the most important pieces of information is the estimated days to maturity. Planting a vegetable in August that will take 90 days to mature is a recipe for disappointment if you're a gardener in the upper Midwest. Similarly, planting flower seed of a cool weather variety in Arizona in February will also almost insure failure. Wise gardeners must calculate the days until harvest by taking average climatic conditions into consideration.

Jesus speaks at length about the seed of faith in the parable of the sower (Matthew 13; Mark 4:1-20; Luke 8:1-15). In the parable of the mustard seed, He describes the amount of faith needed to truly follow Him and bring about the Kingdom of Heaven (Matthew 13:31-32; Mark 4:30-32; Luke 13:18-21). Seeds of faith may hold the promise of reaching maturity, even though we have no idea of how much time remains before the "killing frost" ends our earthly life.

Our task as Christians is to press toward a successful "harvest" through faith nurtured in prayer, Scripture study, fasting, worshiping, and joining together in fellowship with other believers (2 Peter 3:18). By doing this, we will bear fruit regardless of how many days to maturity might remain.

This Coming Week

Time is a concept that scientists cannot fully explain. Take time from your busy schedule each day to thank God who is beyond all time and space.

APRIL DEVOTIONS

Contents:

SERVICEBERRY

But the fruit of the Spirit is love, joy, peace, forbearance, kindness, goodness, faithfulness. Galatians 5:22

The early spring appearance of white blossoms in the dull winter-weary Michigan woodlands is a welcome sight. The white serviceberry blossoms burst out from the subdued background of deep green pines and the bare browns and grays of deciduous trees.

The apt-named serviceberry trees not only light up the drab early spring woodlands, but they also provide tiny apple-like fruits that are food for many wildlife species and songbirds. The fruits of these trees are rich in iron, copper, and vitamin C. Native American peoples often dried the small serviceberry fruits, mashed them, and mixed them with meat and fat to form pemmican (the first power bars).

Once the dominant woodland trees such as oaks and maples leaf out, the small serviceberry trees blend into the background. Yet, in their diminutive role, the trees continue to provide food for woodland birds and other animals.

The Lord calls us to service as well. But no matter what our earthly role in the Kingdom of God, we always need to be humbly mindful of how small a tree we are in the mighty forest of God's universe. As Mother Theresa said, "We can do no great thing, only small things with great love." Let us bear whatever tiny fruits of the Spirit we might have for the good of the entire community around us.

Week 1 /Day 2

LITTLE THINGS MATTER

Whoever can be trusted with very little can also be trusted with much, and whoever is dishonest with very little will also be dishonest with much. Luke 16:10

Say's phoebe (named for Thomas Say, the American naturalist) is a beautiful small bird related to flycatchers. It spends winters in the Southwest but ranges as far north as Alaska in summer. This species of phoebe migrates north earlier in the spring than do other birds that rely solely on insects as food. The reason is that Say's phoebes feed close to the ground where the early spring sun has the greatest warming effect. Because of this warming, insect activity begins early and provides needed food for the phoebes. Other flycatchers feed higher in shrubs and trees where the air remains cold and insects remain dormant longer. In the life of a Say's phoebe, as with all of creation, little things matter. In the case of the phoebe, it's the microclimate close to the ground.

In our attempt to follow Christ, it is also often the little things that matter. Most of us will never be called to be missionaries in a foreign land, be a leader in planting a church, or lead thousands to Christ at an outdoor revival. However, most of us at one time or another will be called to comfort a friend in need; to help at a local food bank; or to contribute our time, talent, or treasure to a worthy cause. Our calling is to be available to the cause of Christ in whatever form it appears within our limited circumstances (Matthew 25:21). Taking time to create a microclimate of God's love for those around us is where the strength of our faith lies.

Week 1 /Day 3

CAUTION, DRAINS TO LAKE

Then the righteous will answer him, "Lord, when did we see you hungry and feed you, or thirsty and give you something to drink?" Matthew 25:37

A local scout troop project involved stenciling signs on storm drains along the streets. The design of the sign was a fish with the words printed beneath it, "Caution, drains to lake." The sign was a reminder and warning that anything going into the drain will end up in local streams, rivers, and lakes. Dumping oil, pesticides, paints, and other toxic materials down the drain could have severe adverse impacts on fish and other aquatic life downstream.

The famous naturalist John Muir once said, "Everything is hitched to everything else." Although he made this comment over a hundred years ago, it is an ecological principle we understand more fully every day.

As Christians growing in our faith, there is a need to recognize that our actions and inactions have consequences well beyond the immediate circumstance. Any time goods are purchased from companies that exploit workers or destroy the environment to meet "demand", the demand will require more exploitation and further environmental destruction. Wasting fossil fuels contributes unnecessarily to further adverse climate change. Our everyday eating habits have an impact on our brothers and sisters throughout the world. The more we take from the earth, the less is available for others.

Taking the words of Jesus seriously means continually expanding our understanding of the relatedness of all beings with which we share this planet. There is always a downstream impact from every action. Let us pray that the Lord's words to Ezekiel (34:19) do not apply to our lives of ignorant abundance — "Must my flock feed on what you have trampled and drink what you have muddied with your feet?" There are countless brothers and sisters who are downstream from everything we use and everything we do.

Week 1 /Day 4

MORNING RAINBOW

I have set my rainbow in the clouds, and it will be the sign of the covenant between me and the earth. Genesis 9:13

The first day of the writers' conference I was attending in town was less than inspiring. I felt that I hadn't learned much or been taught anything exciting or new. I wondered whether I had made a good decision to spend the time and money on the conference. In fact, as I got ready to leave for the conference the next morning, I thought about cutting my losses and just staying home. Then I looked out the kitchen window and saw a beautiful rainbow arching through the sky over the little lake near our house.

A rainbow was the sign of the first covenant between God and humankind (Genesis 9:12). In fact, it was a covenant with all living creatures (Genesis 9:15-17), one that has never been rescinded. As the last storm clouds of the Flood receded, the distant raindrops bent the sunlight to form a rainbow, which God uses repeatedly as a reminder to preserve His creation.

The rainbow is also a reminder to us that since the ultimate owner of all creation has promised to preserve life on Earth, we, as God's appointed caretakers of creation, are also obligated to care for and preserve all life on Earth (Psalm 24:1; Genesis 9:17; Genesis 2:15). This is a sacred covenant.

My writing focuses on the various aspects of God's creation, and so the appearance of the rainbow the second morning of the writers' conference was especially significant to me. I went back to the conference and the second day was much more fulfilling. Was it a sign? Perhaps. But it was also a reminder of God's covenant and of our need to care for and nurture the earth and to be grateful for it.

Week 1 /Day 5

EARLY SPRING

Ask the Lord for rain in the springtime; it is the Lord who sends the thunderstorms. He gives showers of rain to all people, and plants of the field to everyone. Zechariah 10:1

Lengthening days, the smell of flowers in the air, and the slight warmth in the breeze give winter-weary Midwest residents that exhilarating feeling that spring may finally be coming. Except for a few sprouting skunk cabbages in marshy areas and maybe some early forsythia blooms, not much may have noticeably changed from winter, but the promise of spring is unmistakable.

Personal difficulties, health issues, changes, and loss in our lives may lead us to believe that we are stuck in a kind of winter. We may feel that spring will never come again. Yet, meditating on God's promises through Scripture and turning to Him in prayer can bring spiritual warmth and a breath of fresh air from the Holy Spirit. The Lord has promised never to leave us or forsake us no matter what (Hebrews 13:5).

If you need a little springtime in your life, turn to the Lord.

This Coming Week

Thank God and pray for all the people that make your life better but to whom you often pay little attention—postal workers, trash collectors, bank tellers, grocery clerks, etc.

Week 2 /Day 1

CAIRNS AND ALTAR STONES

In the future, when your children ask you, "What do these stones mean?" tell them that the flow of the Jordan was cut off before the ark of the covenant of the Lord. Joshua 4:7

Over the years, my wife and I have been involved in prayer hikes. These hikes consist of walking through a natural area and stopping several places along the way. At each stop we read a short passage of Scripture and spent a few minutes in silent prayer. One beautiful fall day, we did a prayer walk with some friends in a park close to our house.

We had to cross a small creek on our return home. It was there we decided to construct a cairn along the creek bank. Each stone placed on the pile was to represent a prayer concern. We knew that eventually rain-swollen creek waters would wash away all evidence of our little structure, just as God's love and grace would eventually wash away the concerns represented by our stones.

In the Old Testament, uncut and natural stones were often used to build temporary altars or to commemorate a particular event. Jacob made a makeshift memorial from the stone he had used as a pillow when God spoke to him in his dream of the Promised Land (Genesis 28:18). God instructed Moses to make altars only of earth or uncut stone for sacrifices (Exodus 20:25), and Joshua had 12 stones from the Jordan's riverbed set up as a memorial to crossing into the Promised Land (Joshua 4:9).

God often speaks to us through an experience in nature. When this happens, we sometimes feel moved to commemorate the event, as did Moses, Jacob, and Joshua. Our little pile of stones along the creek representing prayer concerns was a physical way to remember God's promises, but remembrances might appear in many forms: a journal entry, a pressed flower, a shell, a sketch, or maybe an unusual pebble. It's not necessary to create or keep a memento for prayer to be heard, but such actions can enrich our prayer life and strengthen our faith.

Week 2 /Day 2

FREEDOM

It is for freedom that Christ has set us free. Stand firm, then, and do not let yourselves be burdened again by a yoke of slavery. Galatians 5:3

If aquatic dragonfly nymphs could think, they would have a very difficult time envisioning themselves as the aerial acrobatic adult dragonflies they become. It would seem impossible to swim up out of the mud at the bottom of a lake or pond for a life in the air. The transition can only be made through the miracle of metamorphosis.

As a Christian, I'm so often surrounded by and involved in today's culture that I think my living a life of freedom in Christ is impossible. It seems like I'm held down by the muddy weights of worry, fatigue, and work. I find myself interested in and pursuing the same temporary pleasures as the world at large. As a minister once asked, "Would there be enough evidence in a court of law to convict me as a Christian?" I hesitate to honestly answer.

Transitioning from the bondage of the world to freedom in Christ is widely discussed in the New Testament. The Lord tells us that as long as we are in the world, we will have tribulation. Yet, Jesus goes on to state that we should take heart since He came to overcome the world (John 16:33). Jesus further states that if we are determined to be *in* but not *of* the world, our yoke will be light (Matthew 11:30).

Our submersion in the surrounding culture makes such freedom difficult to imagine, but not impossible to achieve. We can't do it on our own. Only with God's help can we metamorphose out of the miry clay (Psalm 40:2) into freedom of a life in Christ. Let that be our prayer.

Week 2 /Day 3

SIGN STIMULI

Then will appear the sign of the Son of Man in heaven. And then all the peoples of the Earth will mourn when they see the Son of Man coming on the clouds of heaven, with power and great glory. Matthew 24:30

I was mobbed by cherry-faced meadow hawks (red dragonflies) as I stopped to look across a small lake near our house. The insects were attracted to the bright red jacket I was wearing. Apparently, they were investigating this huge "dragonfly" that suddenly appeared on the shoreline! Animal behaviorists would refer to the red color as a sign stimulus — something that releases a particular reaction in animals. A wide variety of sign stimuli are known among many species of animals. The open mouth of a baby bird triggers feeding behavior in the parents and ants regurgitate nectar to nest mates in response to certain tapping patterns on their antennae.

We humans have also learned to respond to many signs surrounding us. There are warning signs such as stop signs and traffic lights, directional signs along roadways and inside buildings, and informational signs on businesses and billboards.

The cross is a sign of God's enduring love (John 3:15), but it is also a sign of warning: anyone not willing to bear their cross for Christ cannot be His disciple (Luke 14:27). It is a sign of direction—we need to keep our eyes on Jesus (Hebrews 12:2). For nonbelievers the cross may be seen as foolishness (1 Corinthians 1:18) and a stumbling block (1 Corinthians 1:23).

For Christians, the cross should release in us a sense of awe, gratitude, and adoration for Jesus. It should be the "bright red jacket" that draws us to Christ in times of spiritual dryness and serves as a sign of hope in our occasions of unbelief (Mark 9:24).

Week 2 /Day 4

MEXICAN GOLDPOPPIES

He has made everything beautiful in its time. Ecclesiastes 3:11

The winter rains had been plentiful in the Sonoran Desert, and the early spring desert was ablaze with carpets of Mexican gold poppies, lupines, and other wildflowers. I was eager to get out and photograph some areas where I knew the poppies would be thick. As usual, the day seemed to fly and it was mid-afternoon by the time I got out to the desert.

When I arrived, I was disappointed. While the poppies were thick, their golden colors were subdued. They had begun to close their blossoms for the night, which I later discovered poppy flowers tend to do. Only when exposed to bright sunlight do the flowers open and reveal their full potential beauty.

Human beings are each made in the image of God with the potential for a likeness of God. As an image of God, we are capable of physically representing God to the world—even if it's a poor representation. When we come into the sunlight of God's grace and love, we come closer to being both the image AND likeness of our Savior. Like the sunlight shining on the poppies, we need daily exposure to Jesus's 'Sonlight' before God's beauty can fully reveal itself in us.

Week 2 / Day 5

SWALLOWS

Even the sparrow has found a home, and the swallow a nest for herself where she may have her young—a place near your altar. Psalm 84:3.

All summer, swallows swoop and dive over the surface of the lake near our house. They are in a never-ending search for insect prey, their primary nutrition. The birds seem to expend large amounts of energy in constant flying, and since their prey is mostly invisible from a distance, it's almost as if the birds get energy from thin air.

The same can be said for some people's lives. Looking at their busyness, it's a wonder where they get their energy. Some seem to be purposely on the go, always doing something or needing to be somewhere. Others seem to be energized from a love of what they're doing. Yet others may be keeping busy due to loneliness or boredom. To always be doing and going gives the illusion of a full life.

As followers of Christ, we draw sustenance from Him in order to keep our spiritual energy going day by day. We should not let the busyness of our physical lives interfere with spending time "near the altar." Spiritually, we fly with the Holy Spirit, feeding upon and becoming empowered continually by the Word.

This Coming Week

Stay aware of God's abundant grace available to you every day. We are blessed beyond what we deserve.

Week 3 /Day 1

WATERED FROM BELOW

He will be like a tree planted by the water that sends out its roots by the stream. Jeremiah 17:8 ESV

My flower box has a water reservoir in the bottom that can be filled through a spout. In this way, the flowers are watered from below rather than from above. This reduces evaporation from the flower box soil and encourages the flowers to grow deeper roots. Plants in this kind of flower box can better withstand the hot sun and drying winds of summer.

As Christians, we need to grow our roots deep into the reservoir of Christ's love. A faith unsupported by prayer will easily die in the face of adversity. By our examination of conscience, our regular meeting with other Christians for worship, and fasting, our roots will grow deep and strong. Without those practices, we become like the seed that fell on rocky ground only to dry up and blow away (Matthew 13:5).

If the living water of Christ's love seems much further below the surface than our faith roots have grown, there's only one way to reach it—spiritual discipline.

Week 3 /Day 2

MAILBOX OWNERSHIP

The land must not be sold permanently, because the land is mine and you are but aliens and tenants. Leviticus 25:23 NRSV

For many years, a song sparrow nested in a juniper bush by our mailbox. The male sparrow would entertain my wife and me for weeks during the spring and summer by sitting on top of the mailbox post singing his heart out. We were always amused about how, as far as the sparrow was concerned, he owned the territory surrounding his mailbox perch.

The sparrow's territorial behavior made me think how laughable we are in our illusion of ownership of what God alone owns (Psalm 24:1). In our Western culture, we take our property ownership very seriously, and insist on our rights to do with our property as we please. To a large degree, we have lost sight of God's ultimate ownership of everything—including the land.

As mentioned in Genesis 1:29-30, the land is His gift to humanity, and He expects us to care for it. As first stated in Genesis 2:15, we are caretakers only of God's Earth. We are but aliens and tenants on God's land (Leviticus 25:23). Come to think of it, we don't own any more of creation than do song sparrows!

Week 3 /Day 3

MOREL MUSHROOM HUNTING

The Kingdom of Heaven is like treasure hidden in a field, which someone found and hid; then in his joy he goes and sells all that he has and buys that field. Matthew 13:44 NRSV

"Mushroom" isn't a word found in the Bible. The dry lands and deserts of the Middle East aren't abundant with these fungi (although maybe a few grow in the Lebanon mountains around the cedars!).

In the Midwest, we have morel mushrooms, sometimes in great abundance, which tend to grow near certain kinds of trees both living and dead. Some mushroom hunters revisit the same locations each year where they have found an abundance of morels. Often these locations are in woodlots or in forested areas that the mushroom hunters do not own. As a result, these locations are kept secret.

In the parable of the hidden treasure, a field is purchased, but the kingdom, not the field, is the treasure. The man discovers the treasure and the joy it brings, but he can only enjoy it secretly until he gives up all his worldly possessions to become the owner of the field. Freed from needing to hide his treasure, he can enjoy its blessings without fear of losing access. Sacrifice was needed to obtain the treasure.

We live in a culture where there's an attempt to put a price on everything—even people. Still there are things that cannot be bought, such as true peace and joy. These fruits of the spirit must be searched for diligently. We may occasionally taste of these treasures, but to truly possess them in our daily lives each of us must determine what obstacles must be "sold off" in order to obtain them.

Week 3 /Day 4

PRIORITIES

Finish your outdoor work and get your fields ready: after that, build your house. Proverbs 24:27

Springtime is always a very busy time for gardeners like me. With the arrival of warmer temperatures, plant life quickly shifts into high gear and presents a lot of demands for a successful gardening season. Tilling the soil, sowing seeds, transplanting seedlings, weeding, and regular watering are just some of the jobs requiring attention. These outdoor jobs become a priority in early spring when I often must leave unfinished winter projects in the house.

The idea of setting priorities (since time waits for no one) reminds me of my daily struggle in starting my day with some time with the Lord. I often let the pressures of the day push morning devotional time out of the way. In a sense, I go to work immediately on the "house" while letting the "fields" go. I need to remind myself that time moves on and ever closer to the time of God's harvest when my little house projects will be meaningless compared to fields planted with prayer and love for all of God's children.

Week 3 /Day 5

NIGHT WATCH

Praise the Lord, all you servants of the Lord who minister by night in the house of the Lord. Psalm 134:1

The last several years, I have volunteered to monitor frog activity in nearby wetlands. The effort is part of an international program to gauge the health of waters surrounding the Great Lakes. Volunteers go to set locations three different nights from April through July and record the frog species that are calling.

Some of God's creatures—such as spring peepers, chorus frogs, toads, green frogs, and bullfrogs — keep the night watch. As summer progresses, the amphibian nighttime chorus is joined by crickets, cicadas, katydids, and tree crickets. Bird song in the daytime acts as praise lifted to the Creator, but the frogs and insects show that sunset doesn't end the praises coming from God's beautiful and diverse creatures.

Psalm 148 calls upon followers to praise the Lord, and Paul exhorts continual prayer and praise to the Lord in all circumstances. Getting into the habit of nightly prayer and praising the Creator before falling asleep can help calm body and soul. It is then possible to rest assured, knowing that somewhere on Earth, God's nighttime creatures will continue the praises until dawn.

This Coming Week

Spend some time this week thinking about some of the obstacles in your life that may be robbing you of joy and peace. Ask the Lord to help you gain freedom these hindrances.

Week 4 /Day 1

BIRDS OF DIFFERENT FEATHERS

Do not be yoked together with unbelievers. For what do righteousness and wickedness have in common? Or what fellowship can light have with darkness? 2 Corinthians 6:14

Several cormorants were hanging out at the little lake by my Michigan home all spring. Usually, they just pass through on migration, but apparently the fishing was better this time around than in previous years. Every morning the cormorants sat on some stumps and dead limbs along the bank, and every morning a solitary, much smaller Lesser Scaup paddled around in the water next to them.

Although the scaup probably remained near the cormorants for protection, I began to wonder if the scaup possibly identified itself as a cormorant. Remaining close to the cormorants during spring and summer may have seemed like a smart move for the scaup, but when the larger birds left the lake in the fall to migrate south, the smaller bird was left alone, without protection. It had none of its own kind to follow south in migration.

The experience reminded me of Paul's admonition about "being unequally yoked," which is often interpreted as referring to marriages between believers and unbelievers, although Paul did not specifically refer to marriage. The passage can be broadly interpreted as a warning to remind yourself in all circumstances of who might share in your life of faith. As followers of Christ, you should avoid relationships that will be detrimental to your Christian faith. These relationships could be of a personal, business, religious, or other nature. This does not mean avoiding others with different beliefs or views, but it does mean not entering binding relationships that will cause you to compromise your faith.

Week 4 /Day 2

STRATIGRAPHY

Man puts his hand to the flinty rock and overturns mountains by the roots. Job 28:9 ESV

In geology, stratigraphy is the study of rock layers to determine the Earth's history. In archeology, the term relates to studying layers of soil and artifacts laid down over the centuries by one civilization building upon the ruins of another. Obviously, the purpose of these studies is to gain knowledge and understanding of past events.

When I look back at my life, I can study the stratigraphic layers that have resulted in who I am at this instant in life. The layered influences of parents, friends, teachers, spouse, bosses, places, pains, joys, successes, and disappointments have shaped me into the person I am. With eyes of faith, I can examine where God has worked through all these layers of my life even though at the time, I could have cared less about what God was doing.

Of course, we learn from our past, but it is still "past," and we should learn as the poet Stanley Kunitz wrote in his poem "Layers'— "to live in the layers and not in the litter" of our lives. We can gain understanding looking at the past, but wisdom to live life in our current layer and into the future only comes from fear of the Lord — not a fear of retribution, but a fear based on *awe*, as Job describes. Going forward in a life with Christ, we have confidence that we are ever-new creations.

Week 4 /Day 3

REST ASSURED

Though you lie down among the sheepfolds, you will be like the wings of a dove covered with silver, and her feathers with yellow gold. Psalm 68:13

Shepherds of biblical times constructed sheepfolds of brush and briars as temporary nighttime structures for protection of the sheep. The shepherds also often had a hut for themselves within the sheepfold, for their own comfort and protection.

My wife and I have been married over 50 years, and for most nights through all those years together we have taken turns saying nighttime prayers. These prayers sometimes seem rather boring or perfunctory, but we persist in them nonetheless and are comforted building this nightly "sheepfold" of prayer before sleep.

Although I seem to have a more difficult time now than when I was younger, I have always viewed going to bed as putting away the cares and concerns of the day. I visualize the angels of the Lord standing watch, which, while maybe a little juvenile, is a very comforting thought.

Psalm 68 suggests that even as we rest within God's sheepfold, His saving mercies continue. While there are many different interpretations of verse 13, in which words like "pots," "lots," and "campfires" are used rather than "sheepfolds," I love the idea of having God's protection as I sleep and as He continues administering His saving grace.

Week 4 /Day 4

I GOT A NAME

Fear not, for I have redeemed you; I have summoned you by name; you are mine. Isaiah 43:1

As I walk through the fields and woods, I like to be able to name the plants and animals I encounter. Knowing a common name gives me a sense of understanding what I see, however limited my knowledge. I may not know the scientific genus and species names, but a common name is good enough for me.

Names are important for identifying and providing a means to associate characteristics of a person, place, or thing. God helped Adam to better understand the world surrounding him when He brought the animals to him for naming (Genesis 2:19). The Bible tells us that during the time of Enoch (Adam's grandson through Seth), people began to call upon the name of the Lord (Genesis 4:26), and the third commandment warns against misuse of God's name (Genesis 20:7). God changed Jacob's name to Israel (Genesis 35:10), an angel told Zechariah to name his son John (Luke 1:13), and Gabriel told Mary to name her Son Jesus (Luke 1:31).

Several years ago, the late Jim Croce wrote the song "I Got a Name." In the first verse there is a simple statement that, like the pine tree and toad, I have a name—I'm known, and I have worth. In our culture of increasing anonymity and dehumanization, we need to keep in mind the importance of every individual—each of the more than 8 billion of us are known intimately and loved by God. As the praise song says, "He knows my name."

Week 4 /Day 5

DESERT INCENSE

And the smoke of the incense, with the prayers of the saints, rose before God from the hand of the angel. Revelation 8:4

Brittlebush is a native shrub of the Sonoran Desert. After a fall and winter of adequate rainfall, brittlebushes bloom profusely with bright yellow flowers that blanket the washes and lower slopes of the desert mountains. Friars in early Spanish missions called the plant "inciensio" after they discovered that when burned, the dried resin of the brittlebush had an aroma similar to frankincense.

The sense of smell is stronger and more linked to our sense of taste and to our memories than any of the four other senses. Since the burning of incense involves the sense of smell, it is not any surprise that it has been used for thousands of years in Judeo-Christian traditions. Whether it's frankincense or brittlebush resin, incense in the air can serve as both a symbolic offering and as a reminder of God's holiness. One of my favorite passages is Revelation 5:8 where the 24 elders surrounding the Lamb "were holding golden bowls full of incense, which are the prayers of the saints."

What a powerful and beautiful vision—our prayers becoming incense offered by the elders at the feet of the Lamb of God! Although the burning of incense might somehow assist us in our physical worship of the Lord by involving our sense of smell, our prayers offered in love to our Lord at any time and in any place will join with those of all the saints in offering a continual and beautiful fragrance to the Lord.

The Coming Week:

Say a short nightly prayer of thanksgiving for the day and for God's presence with you as you sleep.

MAY DEVOTIONS

Contents:

Week 1 /Day 1

EXTRAVAGANT ABUNDANCE

The grace of the Lord was poured out on me abundantly, along with the faith and love that are in Christ Jesus. 1 Timothy 1:14

For many years my wife and I owned a house surrounded by numerous silver maple trees. Every spring the trees produced massive numbers of seeds we referred to as keys. In May thousands of keys would fall from the trees, spinning around like little helicopters in the wind and landing all over the yard, flowerbeds, and garden. Soon little maple seedlings would start popping up everywhere: in the yard (only to be mowed down), in the rows of garden lettuce to be hoed out, or in the street to be washed away by the next rain. Of course, a few landed in the nearby woods, giving promise of new mature silver maples in the years ahead.

In the parable of the sower (Luke 8:4-8, 11-15), Jesus emphasizes what happens to the seeds as they fall on rocky ground, among weeds, on the path, or on good ground. However, there is also something about the sower that can be discerned in the parable. He is broadcasting seeds all over the place with apparent abandon. This is like the maple that takes no care in where the seeds fall but produces prodigiously. So too does God, the sower, sow prodigiously and with exuberant extravagance. His grace falls on everyone, and even if grace falling on a life at first doesn't immediately bear fruit, God keeps showering it down. This happens day after day and year after year just as the maple trees drop keys. Look up right now, seeds of grace are falling on your life.

Week 1 /Day 2

LOOSE SANDALS

Who may ascend the hill of the Lord? Who may stand in his holy place? Psalm 24:3 NRSV

Our dog, Mayzi, enjoyed her morning walks along the street by our house. There was a steep hill at the end of the street. I named the rise "the holy hill" and often stopped there for a short prayer time.

One summer morning, as Mayzi and I were coming down from the holy hill, one of my sandal straps broke. I had no means to repair it, but I also could not walk with it flapping off my foot. I tried walking with one sandal on and one sandal off, but that wasn't any better. I ended up having to take off both sandals and walked home barefoot on the street. The return home was a much more mindful walk than usual, with tender feet contacting pavement, stones, and grit.

This little incident reminded me of when Moses spoke to God by way of the burning bush, and God instructed him to take off his sandals because he was standing on holy ground (Exodus 3:5). It is a good lesson. We have so insulated ourselves with our cars, homes, and even our shoes that we seldom physically experience the holiness of all His creation. This disregard also makes it easier to profane and pollute it.

God has given us a uniquely beautiful earthly home that we need to care for, as He instructed us (Genesis 2:15). We need to confess and repent of those things we are doing in both our personal lives and as a society that damage God's holy ground. Taking off our shoes and contacting God's Earth—or the pavement we've poured over it—can be a good exercise in creation care awareness.

Week 1 /Day 3

CRYPTOBIOTIC

He will respond to the prayer of the destitute; He will not despise their plea. Psalm 102:17

In the deserts of the West, appearances can be deceiving. During dry periods, the soil seems brown and lifeless. However, after a rain the soil surface often acquires a greenish and/or reddish tint. This change in appearance is a result of a complex mix of tiny organisms that make up what is called "cryptobiotic soil." In Latin, "crypto" means hidden, and "bio" refers to life. "Hidden life," describes these organisms well. The thin layers of bacteria, algae, mosses, and lichens on the desert soil surface are essential to desert life since they stabilize and add nutrients to the soil.

Sometimes when I look around at the world it seems like God is "crypto"—hidden and out of sight. When bad things happen, many ask, "Where is God?" Even the psalmists cried out in anguish wondering where God was in their time of need (Psalm 4:1, Ps 10:1).

In those moments of His seeming absence, I am reminded of a quote from Edmund Burke: "Never despair, but if you do, work on in despair." That is, sometimes we must seek the Lord, by praying on in despair. Our tears shed in prayer will be like rain on the desert soil, transforming the illusion of lifeless surroundings and hopelessness into a reality of new life and beauty.

Week 1 /Day 4

DOING FIELD WORK WITH THE LORD

Do you have eyes but fail to see, and ears but fail to hear? And don't you remember? Mark. 8:18

I have a friend who is a great naturalist. Dave knows just about every bit of flora and fauna he encounters and often can identify birds by their calls alone. Being out in nature with Dave opens my eyes and ears to things I would never perceive without someone pointing them out. Dave's kind of knowledge of the natural world was achieved by spending a lot of time in the field, as well as studying guides and other information about the plants and animals encountered. It is not something easily learned in a few days, but rather is the result of a lifetime of dedication and experience.

Truly seeing the Lord at work in our lives, trying to grasp the concept of the Kingdom of Heaven, and hearing what the Lord might have to say is a lifetime endeavor. It requires time in the field (with the Lord in prayer), plus on-going study of his field manual—the Bible. Without such commitment, we become like the Jews that Jesus spoke of in Matthew 13:14 and in Mark 4:12: "Though seeing, they do not see; though hearing, they do not hear or understand."

God is present in our lives and all around us, but we must put in the work to know Him. Studying the field manual, spending time alone and with other "naturalists" in prayer—as well as finding an experienced mentor—can greatly aid our spiritual perception.

Week 1 /Day 5

USEFUL JUNK

All who cleanse themselves of the things I have mentioned will become special utensils, dedicated and useful to the owner of the house, ready for every good work. 2 Timothy 2:21

My wife and I are blessed with the view of a small lake from our condo. One spring day we noticed a small piece of floating wood caught among some emergent weeds along the shoreline. It didn't seem like much of anything—just a piece of junk floating in the water. However, later in the day, we saw a muskrat crawl out of the water onto the piece of wood. The muskrat sat there for a while resting and scratching himself before sliding back into the water. A few days later, two painted turtles were taking advantage of the same piece of driftwood. They had also found this floating platform and were sunning themselves in the early spring sunlight.

Sometimes we all feel like trash caught in the weeds of life, but as the saying goes, "God doesn't make junk." The greatest message of Christianity is that the Creator of the universe loves us. Even if we feel broken or discounted by the world around us, we are not forgotten by God. He loves us, and we can be of use to Him right where we are, in the same way that a lowly piece of wood was put to good use by creatures in the pond.

This Coming Week

Remember that regardless of circumstances God's grace continues to be available to you every minute of the day.

Week 2 /Day 1

STORIES IN THE SAND

If any one of you is without sin, let him be the first to throw a stone at her. Again He stooped down and wrote on the ground. John 8:7-8 NRSV

I recently took a walk along a Lake Michigan beach and started listing whatever I observed at the water's edge. Objects included gull feathers, charred wood, water-smoothed driftwood, zebra mussel shells, wings of dead Monarch butterflies, plastic caps and bottles, cigarette butts, and flip-flops. These objects constructed a kind of story in the sand. The charred wood, plastic trash, cigarette butts, and flip-flops told a story of people partying on the beach. The gull feathers told of handouts and edible trash. Zebra mussel shells testified to the unwanted presence of an invasive species in the Great Lakes, and the Monarch wings reminded us that long-distance migrations can turn deadly.

The most important sand story mentioned in the Bible is in John 8:1-11 where, while confronting the Pharisees on whether to stone an adulteress, Jesus wrote something in the sand. What he wrote was not recorded, but it played a big role in His lesson on forgiveness and in defusing the call of the self-righteous Pharisees to stone the woman. Jesus's message in the sand was undoubtedly soon obliterated, but the people He touched by the story left behind were undoubtedly changed—hopefully for good.

We walk this Earth but for a brief while, and the physical remnants of our walk eventually become obliterated by the drifting sands of time. But the love and forgiveness we share with one another in Jesus's name will continue into eternity. Like Jesus, let's be more concerned with writing love into people's hearts than with writing our own stories in the sand.

Week 2 /Day 2

GATHER AND SCATTER

There is a time for everything, and a season for every activity under heaven: a time to scatter stones and a time to gather them. Ecclesiastes 3:5

Sandhill cranes gather by the thousands on marshes they have returned to for eons, V-shaped formations of geese annually wing south together, and herds of elk move together to grasslands at lower elevations every winter. These are just a few of the great annual fall migrations of animals in the Northern Hemisphere. During these times, individual animals join others of their kind with the common goals of survival and security. These same animals will later separate from each other to establish territories, find mates, and raise young.

The Christian life also cycles between gathering and scattering, inward and outward. We gather for praise and worship, for mutual support, love, and accountability; and we scatter to spread the love of Christ into the world around us. Paul emphasized the need for believers to meet for worship and support (Hebrews 10:25), just as Jesus charged the disciples to go and preach the good news to all the world (Mark 16:15). Our faith may not survive without regular contact with fellow believers, but we also can't be bearers of the Good News without leaving the safety and comfort of our Christian community and taking the light of Jesus into the world. Balance between the two is the Christian goal.

Week 2 /Day 3

GOOD BIRDS

But even the hairs of your head are all counted. Do not be afraid; you are of more value than many sparrows. Matthew 10:30-31 NRSV

I recently joined a group of experienced bird watchers from the local Audubon society on a field trip. Such trips always have a leader and a recorder who writes down all the species seen or heard by members of the group. I found it interesting that common birds like blackbirds, goldfinches, and cardinals were usually just called out and recorded without comment. If a Cooper's hawk, chestnut-sided warbler, or some other more unusual bird was spotted, the leader or recorder would often compliment whoever first located the bird with the comment "good bird." In other words, the unusual birds were good and the common birds were—well, just common.

This sort of classification of *good vs. no comment* made me think how we classify and judge people. How do we define common? Common is seen as the everyday—unremarkable, and certainly nothing miraculous. We are lulled into taking common people and the world around us for granted, barely worthy of note.

Fortunately for us, this is not the way God views His creation. We are each special in God's eyes, miracles of life. As the psalmist states in Psalm 139, "I praise you because I am fearfully and wonderfully made." If we think we are just common because of the way we look, or because of what we do, or what we have, or anything else measured by the world, remember what God told Samuel, "The Lord does not look at the things man looks at." (1 Samuel 16:7)

God does not distinguish between good birds and common birds, just as Jesus did not die for good people, common people, bad people, or any other classification of human beings. He died equally for all. He loves you just the way you are. It's your decision to love Him back.

Week 2 /Day 4

DIFFERENCES IN PERCEPTION

Go to the ant, you sluggard; consider its ways to be wise. Proverbs 6:6

Insects are the most abundant creatures in God's creation, but most people have little appreciation for the variety and vast numbers of insect species that share the planet with us. Scientists have described about 900 thousand insect species and estimate that millions more await discovery. Incredibly, the weight of all insects living at any one time is greater than that of all other terrestrial animals combined.

Insects are biologically successful because they are small and can find many niches in which to live. Many also have the capability to fly, giving them great mobility for their size. An insect's perception of the world and experiences in it are quite different from our own. Many insects can see the world in ultraviolet light, some taste with their feet, others find their way using the scent of chemicals called pheromones. It's also hard to imagine what an exoskeleton rather than an internal skeleton would feel like.

It's not likely, however, that insects are aware of their miraculous existence. Unlike insects, our perception of the world around us is shaped not only by our senses but also by our ability to be aware of what it means to be alive. God has given us a capability of sensing His presence and sharing His love. We can taste and see that the Lord is good (Psalm 34:8) when we perceive the wisdom of His ways (Proverbs 9:4), through our encounter with the world.

Week 2 /Day 5

HUMUS, HUMANS, HUMILITY, AND HUMOR

Do nothing out of selfish ambition or vain conceit, but in humility consider others better than yourselves. Philippians 2:3 NRSV

Humus is that wonderfully dark, rich, crumbly soil full of nutrients for plant growth sought after by gardeners. Humans are that wonderfully complex, multi-colored creation formed by God out of dust (Genesis 2:7). Both have great potential. Unfortunately, much human potential has been lost due to a lack of humility. Because of arrogance and ignoring the instructions of God, humans have been condemned to a life of hard work and an eventual return to becoming humus (Genesis 3:19). A lack of humility seems to be our continual downfall as a race.

Still, just as gardeners seek out humus God continues to seek us out for our potential. If we truly know where we stand in relationship to God and to our fellow human beings, we will "inherit the Earth" and "enjoy great peace" (Psalm 37:11 and Matthew 5:5). Through true humility, we can become a kind of spiritual humus that encourages others to grow spiritually and follow Jesus—the ultimate example of humility (Philippians 2:4-8).

As any gardener knows, you don't waste good humus by using it on garden paths to walk on. Humus has too many valuable benefits for the garden, and it needs to be worked in among the crops where its giving nature results in good fruits. This is what the Lord will do with us in humility—work us into our surroundings to produce His good fruit. With that in mind, we can start to live a full and humble life for Christ assured that God is smiling on us and not laughing at our folly (Psalm 37:13).

This Coming Week

Reflect on how we all are guilty of judging those around us.

Week 3 /Day 1

KETTLE LAKES

The good leave an inheritance to their children's children, but the sinner's wealth is laid up for the righteous. Proverbs 13:22 NRSV

I enjoy fishing in the many lakes near our home in the upper Midwest, but I never realized their origin until I heard the term "kettle lakes." Many of the lakes in this part of the country formed as the last of the continental glaciers receded about 10,000 years ago. Large chunks of ice would sometimes break off from the receding front of the glacier and would form deep depressions in the Earth. These ice chunks would be left behind to slowly melt, leaving new-formed kettle lakes. The lakes are a lasting impression of the once mighty ice sheet.

I wonder what kind of lasting impression my life will leave as I recede towards my own end. As a parent and grandparent, I hope that I will leave a few beautiful "kettle lakes"—a good impression that will provide evidence of my faith in the Lord. There are times when I don't feel that I'm really living up to this goal. It seems easier to just provide things or attention to my grandkids than to help them witness God's love. Still, I pray that I will improve in pointing them towards lakes of living water that they will be able to access throughout their lives, both in times of need and in times of joy.

AUTOIMMUNE DISEASE

And can any of you by worrying add a single hour to your span of life? Matthew 6:27 NRSV

My wife has indications of possible autoimmune disease although it hasn't yet been completely diagnosed. Autoimmune diseases such as rheumatoid arthritis, lupus, and Crohn's disease affect millions of people worldwide. In each case, a person's own immune system attacks certain internal tissues or organs, creating disease.

Many more people, including myself, suffer from a type of mental autoimmune disease, called *worry*. We make ourselves miserable and even generate physical illness through excessive worry. Anxiety is rampant in a culture of immediate news flashes over the Internet and social media responding to daily acts of violence, financial insecurity, and political turmoil.

Jesus taught repeatedly that it is futile to worry about what we might eat, drink, or wear, as well as what to say or think. We have no control over many things. Yet most of us know that it's very difficult not to worry since worries often reflect where our hearts are most of the time—in pursuit of superficial desires (money, prestige, and getting ahead).

With God's help, it is possible to heal from the autoimmune effects of worry. Through prayer, increased faith and action we can turn away from worldly goals and accept a healthy freedom in Christ.

Week 3 /Day 3

PHLOEM AND XYLEM

Through Jesus, therefore, let us continually offer to God a sacrifice of praise—the fruit of lips that openly profess his name. Hebrews 13:15

When I was a kid, our family took a 10,000-mile journey around the western half of the United States. Although I have many memories of that trip of more than 60 years ago, I will always remember standing in a California redwood grove. Some of the majestic trees with their gigantic trunks rose over 300 feet towards the sky.

Water picked up by the roots of these giants is conveyed up the xylem beneath the trunk bark all the way to the leaves or needles in the tree canopy. It's there in every living needle that the miracle of photosynthesis combines water with carbon dioxide in the presence of sunlight to create sugars and other foods needed for the tree's growth. This food then travels down the phloem tubes back to the tree roots to nourish the tree.

As Christians, we offer up prayers and praise like water flowing up through tree xylem to the leaves. God takes these and transforms them with His 'Sonlight' into the spiritual food we need.

Week 3 /Day 4

HELPFUL OR UNHELPFUL?

All things are lawful for me, but not all things are beneficial. All things are lawful for me, but I will not be dominated by anything. 1 Corinthians. 6:12

One Saturday several years ago, our neighbor Dave and I were talking as a mass emergence of 17-year cicadas was peaking in the neighborhood. I told Dave I had heard that cicadas were edible and that they supposedly had a somewhat caramel-like taste raw. I then picked up a newly emerged cicada and ate it. It tasted awful, and I ended up with a mildly upset stomach the rest of the day. Since then, I have assumed the true locusts (which are not cicadas) that John the Baptist ate must have tasted better, or maybe he roasted them first!

My stupid action of eating a cicada reminded me of Paul's statement in 1 Corinthians 6:12 and 10:23, that although things may be permissible, they might not be helpful to me or to those around me. There are many things that we as Christians may do that may seem fine at first but turn out to be a detriment to ourselves or others.

For one example, I think of the broad acceptance of wine drinking among our family and friends. Although moderate consumption is not prohibited in Scripture, serving alcohol at a small family gathering where there is a recovering alcoholic present is certainly not helpful. For another example, I like to fish and, for most people, fishing itself is a morally neutral activity, but if I go to fish camp for a month every year and leave my home responsibilities entirely to my wife—that may not be helpful!

As Christians, we need to think about any consequences before we bite into our cicadas. Yes, we have great freedom in Christ, but that freedom also demands great responsibility, not only for ourselves but also for those around us.

A NIGHT CALL

Even the stork in the sky knows her appointed seasons, and the dove, the swift and the thrush observe the time of their migration. But my people do not know the requirements of the Lord. Jeremiah 8:7

White-winged doves spend the winter in Mexico and Central America and migrate into the Desert Southwest in the spring when the saguaro cacti bloom. I learned firsthand that these doves can be very loud, especially when heard early in the morning and coming from right outside a bedroom window. On one occasion I woke up to a dove calling at three in the morning. The bird kept me awake for almost an hour with its continued singing.

Later I thought how I had wasted my loss of sleep in frustration when I could have made it a time of prayer and listening for the Lord. I recalled how God woke Samuel to his calling as a prophet in the middle of the night (1 Samuel 3:1-21). Instead of thinking how I was being robbed of sleep, I could have said as Samuel did, "Speak Lord, your servant is listening."

I've found that with age, I've become a lighter sleeper and often wake up for extended periods during the night. Instead of wasting these times I'm determined to make them a sacred time of listening quietly in the presence of the Lord--even if there's loud bird right outside my window at the time.

This Coming Week

Examine your motives for doing whatever you do this week. How much selfishness is involved?

Week 4 /Day 1

JUMPING OUT IN FAITH

"Alas, Sovereign Lord," I said, "I do not know how to speak; I am too young." Jeremiah 1:6

Unlike many other species of ducks, the natural nesting sites for wood ducks are in tree cavities. The openings to these tree holes can be up to 70 feet above the ground. The mother duck calls to her ducklings from the ground or a nearby tree when the ducklings are just a few days old. Upon hearing their mother, the ducklings jump up the inside walls of the nest cavity clinging to the sides with the tiny claws on their feet. Once they reach the opening, they jump feet first and flap their undeveloped wings. The ducklings often bounce upon hitting the ground, but are usually perfectly fine, and are ready to follow their mother to the nearest water.

In our own immature faith, we often try to live inside our safe and sound "tree holes," but a fully lived life of faith can't be experienced inside a nest. In fact, just as wood ducklings that can't make it out of the hole eventually die, our faith can also die if never tested and exercised. The Lord calls us out of our holes to follow Him, and that means we may have to take a long, scary jump. The Bible relates numerous times when humans have tried to not "jump." When God called, Moses's excuse was poor speaking ability (Exodus 4:10), Isaiah had unclean lips (Isaiah 6:5), and Jeremiah saw himself as too immature (Jeremiah 1:6). Yet each eventually made the leap.

As followers of Christ, we are all called to witness or serve in some capacity. Although we're all capable of finding excuses not to respond to the Lord's call, the only way to a life of faith is to listen for the Word and jump.

Week 4 /Day 2

THE BOOK OF CREATION

For since the creation of the world, God's invisible qualities—his eternal power and divine nature—have been clearly seen, being understood from what has been made so that people are without excuse. Romans 1:20

My more conservative Christian friends sometimes look a little askance at my interest in seeing lessons through God's general revelation—nature. I guess they think such interest could lead to pantheism, where I start circling trees and chanting with crystals.

The danger of idolatry associated with nature worship seems to be the basis for many Christians not taking the time to learn from God's book of general revelation. Yet many other false idols embedded in our culture and worshiped (money, sex, youth, and power) go largely unquestioned.

We humans do have a penchant for turning things into gods. The Old Testament is filled with accounts of God's chosen people putting their faith in the wrong places. Hezekiah even had to destroy the bronze snake that Moses had made in the desert because the people had started worshiping it (2 Kings 18:4)!

Creation is not God, but it is the manifestation of both an immanent and a transcendent God. It is the book of general revelation, which, along with Scripture, teaches us about its Creator. As Paul states in Romans 1:20, creation reflects God's eternal power and divine nature.

If you're not looking into God's book of general revelation regularly, you're missing blessings and an understanding of God found nowhere else. Take time with Scripture in hand to also read the book of creation.

Week 4 /Day 3

CONFLUENCE

But there the Lord in majesty will be for us, a place of broad rivers and streams where no galley with oars can go, nor stately ship can pass. Isaiah 33:21 NRSV

It's networks of creeks, streams, and smaller rivers flowing together that form the mysterious Amazon, the muddy Ohio, the icy Mackenzie, and the mighty Mississippi. The confluences of tributaries both small and large are the lifeblood of these rivers.

Christian worship should be much the same. On the way to the church building where I attend worship, I pass five other churches over the course of about 6 miles. These buildings house tributaries of religious thought that somehow over the centuries have felt the need to set their own pathways to salvation. Instead of joining together to create a powerful river of Christian love flowing through the world, we have chosen to trickle our own ways to the sea.

I often think how much time, talent, and treasure continue to be wasted in duplications of effort to live out the gospels. On rare occasions, multiple denominations will join to address a social or human emergency—often a natural disaster—but then every congregation returns to their own four walls of denominational differences.

I pray we may find confluence and work toward a more ecumenical spirit as tributaries of the Living Water we call Christianity.

Week 4 /Day 4

SUSPENDED IN INFINITY

All the days ordained for me were written in your book before one of them came to be. Psalm 139:16

The bedroom seemed unusually light when I woke around 4:00 a.m. Since there were few artificial lights nearby, I knew it was probably moonlight shining through the blinds. As I lifted the blind to look out across the small pond near our house, I saw the full moon peeking between drifting white clouds. The pond surface was still, perfectly reflecting the beauty of the night sky. The view created a sensation of being suspended in space between two identical skies.

I've often heard the phrase that we are spiritual beings having a human experience. As Christians we tend to think of eternal life as extending from physical death onward. However, the Bible affirms that we have been in the mind of God since the beginning of time. God told Jeremiah: "Before I formed you in the womb, I knew you" (Jeremiah 1:5). Isaiah also acknowledged God's knowledge of him prior to his birth (Isaiah 49:1).

Every one of us is an eternal being suspended in our human body here on this tiny spaceship called Earth for an unbelievably brief moment. And not only that, we are also each known and loved by God who has "had us in mind" from the beginning of the universe. Recognizing this should help us know our true worth and keep the realities of this life in perspective.

Week 4 /Day 5

OBSERATION TOWERS

Lead me to the rock that is higher than I. Psalm 61:2

I have always enjoyed visiting places like state parks, wildlife refuges, and national parks. Observation towers and decks allowing visitors a better view of surrounding landscapes are common in these natural areas. Views from these observation points provide a broader perspective than can be obtained while hiking along a trail through the woods or driving a twisting mountain road that requires the driver's full attention. They also provide a place to rest and think about the beauty of the place.

Prayer can be a lot like an observation tower in our spiritual journey. We can gain a higher perspective of the "landscape" we are traversing through a life of prayer. While we cannot understand any circumstance good or bad in our lives as God understands it, prayer can lift us up above any surrounding obstacles to a "rock that is higher than ourselves." Usually such views are humbling, revealing to us the vast expanses of God's wisdom and mystery and our limited day-to-day perspective.

A view from an observation tower or "higher rock" is always worth the stop.

This Coming Week

Think about how willing or unwilling you are to step out in faith to serve the Lord.

JUNE DEVOTIONS

Contents

June

Week 1 /Day 1

HUMMINGBIRD IRIDESCENSE

But if we walk in the light, as He is in the light, we have fellowship with one another, and the blood of Jesus, his Son, purifies us from all sin. 1 John 1: 7

I recently became interested in bird watching. In addition to size, beak shape, behavior, and general body shape, coloration is very important in bird identification.

Hummingbirds have iridescent feathers; that is, the feathers themselves are not colored but appear colored only because of the way they bend light. I am often struck by how orientation to the sun changes the color of a hummingbird I am watching. The bird appears rather dull and blackish facing away from the sun, but its head and throat flashes bright red when oriented toward the sun.

In the same way, the way our lives are oriented to God makes a difference in how we appear to others. If we keep our eyes on the Lord, the many beautiful colors of His love and mercy will be evident to those around us. If we turn our backs on the Lord, we will lose our "iridescence" along with our ability to point to its source—Jesus our Lord.

Week 1 /Day 2

WEED BOUQUETS

I am my lover's and my lover is mine; he browses among the lilies.
Song of Songs 6:3

My wife loves to gather wildflowers along roadsides and in abandoned fields to make bouquets. There is something about these "lilies of the field" (Matthew 6:28-30) and "browsing among the lilies" (Song of Songs 6:3) that brings joy and creates beauty.

Unlike a garden, where beautiful flowers are often a result of the gardener's knowledge and skill, the wildflowers of the field survive with only God's care, and they are often surprising in their individual colors, abundance, and fragrance. Even many of what are otherwise considered weeds—the invasive, non-native plants—have beauty. But the beauty created when different wildflowers are placed together in a bouquet is a serendipitous celebration of color and form bordering on the miraculous.

God too enjoys picking human "weeds," each one beautiful in its own way, but capable of the miraculous when combined in a bouquet pleasing to Him. The genealogy of Jesus (Matthew 1:1-16) certainly contains some undesirables, such as Tamar, who had to prostitute herself to survive; Rahab, who was also a prostitute; Ruth, the Moabite, who married Boaz; and David, the king and adulterer with Bathsheba.

Jesus too selected from among "weeds" as He assembled His disciples from fishermen, tax collectors, and political zealots. However, the combination of all these weeds culminated in the offer of eternal salvation for all humankind—the most beautiful bouquet ever given to us by our loving Father.

Week 1 /Day 3

LEAVING WAKES

Take my yoke upon you and learn from me, for I am gentle and humble in heart, and you will find rest for your souls. Matthew 11:29

Our canoe left barely a wake as it glided silently across the glassy surface of the lake. Compared to motorized watercraft, canoes are humble vessels, gentle on the environment, and causing little disturbance to water or wildlife. The wake would have been unnoticeable had there been any wind. We were almost as motionless as the dry oak leaves that floated next to us on the water.

In our travels through life, it is impossible not to leave a wake of some kind. We leave some impact on everything and everyone with whom we come into contact—but to what extent? Do we treat people and all of creation gently and with love, or do we leave behind a destructive wake of harshness born of selfishness?

Gentleness is the wake Jesus and His followers left behind. Paul admonished the Ephesians to be humble, gentle, and patient with one another (Ephesians 4:2). He also wrote to Timothy that deacons of the church must be gentle and not violent (1 Timothy 3:3). Peter commended the gentle spirit of women in the early church (1 Peter 3:4).

I know in my own travels that when selfishness surfaces, as it sometimes does, there is little room for gentleness, and people in my wake tend to get hurt. So, I try to be more considerate in my paddling. We all need to look behind occasionally to see what kind of wake we are leaving.

Week 1 /Day 4

RESERVOIRS OF BLESSINGS

Immediately the Spirit sent Him out into the wilderness. Mark. 1:12

The winter and early spring garden appears to be nothing but bare ground with no plants and few signs of life, except a couple of sprouting weeds. Yet as the warm season progresses, vegetables, flowers, and weeds grow, and insect life becomes abundant. Bees visit flowers, preying mantis patrol the cucumbers, and ladybugs munch on aphids.

Where were these creatures during the cold months when the garden was almost lifeless? Most of them cannot survive in the barren, tilled garden; rather, they spend the cold months among the wild, messy unmowed grasses, weeds, and shrubs beyond the garden's edge.

Some blessings come from embracing the wildness of life. After heaven was rent and the Spirit descended at Jesus's baptism, Jesus was driven into the wilderness, where He not only survived but also accepted His mission as suffering servant and not as earthly ruler.

Jesus' ministry had much wildness. He was run out of town, misunderstood by His closest friends, challenged by the religious and cultural establishment, falsely charged and tortured, and deserted as He hung on the cross. However, the wild ride that the Father sent His Son on brought us everlasting life. Thank God for wildness!

Week 1 /Day 5

LIGHT POLLUTION

Praise Him, sun and moon, praise Him all you shining stars. Psalm 148:3

Many people living in urbanized areas rarely see the dark night sky with its billions of stars and the Milky Way streaming from horizon to horizon. Instead, even on clear nights, we see only a few of the brightest stars and planets through a haze of light pollution.

Years ago, our family went camping at Big Bend National Park in West Texas. I will always remember lying on my back on a picnic table looking into the night sky and feeling as though I was falling into the universe itself. I felt close to the Creator.

The lights of our many worldly distractions dim our ability to see the Creator in the creation. In most aspects of our lives, we artificially illuminate the world around us, trying to find our meaning in life without ever being humbled by the vastness of creation and its reflection of God's power and majesty. As David asked in Psalm 8:4, "What is man that Thou are mindful of him?"

By God's grace we have been given a beautiful home in an endless universe. When we truly see the magnificence of the nighttime firmament, there is no response other than praise and thanksgiving for His awesome gifts of beauty and love.

This Coming Week

Pay attention to the many roadside weeds/flowers and read Matthew 6:28

Week 2 /Day 1

WHO'S CALLING?

Beloved, do not believe every spirit, but test the spirits to see whether they are from God; because many false prophets have gone out into the world." 1 John 4:1

With a local Audubon group, I was out checking for various marsh birds as part of an international monitoring program around the Great Lakes. The monitoring procedure consisted of playing recorded calls of various wetland species, and then waiting to see if a bird hidden within the cattail marsh would respond.

Most of the secretive marsh birds that we were looking for were rarely heard and almost never seen. However, one evening, after playing the call of a Virginia Rail, there was not only an audible response, but a diminutive rail actually came creeping out of the marsh. We had tricked the bird into investigating the source of the sound.

Sometimes the world tricks us as well, into following various idols to dead-end paths. Jesus warned of false prophets leading us astray (Matthew 7:15). Paul also warned of the need for discernment (Philippians 1:9-10). Even among believers, there are some who claim that many different trails can lead to the mountaintop. The truth is, there is only one, as Jesus indicated when He said, "I am the way and the truth and the life. No one comes to the Father except through me" (John. 14:6).

Before responding to any calls coming from out in the world, we need to ask ourselves whether it is the one true call, which will bring us closer to Christ and result in advancing His kingdom, or just an imitation.

Week 2 /Day 2

COMMUNION

He is before all things, and in Him all things hold together.
Colossians 1:17

After 9/11, many churches experienced an increase in attendance, as people acknowledged their human frailty and sought comfort in a spiritual community. They felt a need to reconnect with the God of Scripture.

National parks and other natural recreational areas also experienced a sharp increase in visitors after the terrorist attacks, as people sought solace in the quiet strength and beauty of God's creation (whether they acknowledged God as Creator or not).

People who find solace in nature surely experience the immanence of God through general revelation or creation. But those returning to church also experience God's transcendence and the message of hope given through special revelation found in Scripture. To experience God in His wholeness requires both an undergirding of His Word and exposure to His creation.

Christ is both transcendent and immanent. He is present in and holds together all creation moment by moment (Revelation 4:11). We commune with Him through the very acts of breathing, eating, and drinking. Like fish in water, we swim in the presence of Christ and are dependent upon Him for life whether we recognize it or not.

Communion, as observed in Scripture, helps us understand His presence. Through a shared knowledge of Scripture, we can experience the awesome power and majesty of God not only through a historical record of His activity in the Bible but also by physically experiencing the flesh and blood of creation.

Week 2 /Day 3

SOLASTALGIA

God saw everything that He had made, and it was very good. And there was evening and there was morning, the sixth day. Genesis 1:31

"Solastalgia" is a recently coined term created by combining the words "solace," "desolation," and '"nostalgia." It refers to experiencing homesickness while still at home. This sadness can result from environmental changes that somehow severely alter or destroy the feelings associated with one's home place. An example might be Appalachian people surrounded by strip mining operations that have destroyed the surrounding landscape. Another example would be commercial fishermen in Newfoundland, where the fisheries the local people depended on have collapsed.

There is no indication in the Genesis creation story that God ever intended for Adam and Eve to die and leave the paradise on Earth He had created for them. Only after sin entered the picture was earthly paradise lost (Genesis 3:23-24). Our relationship with Earth's Creator was also broken. Humankind began suffering from solastagia—a longing for "home" (the original earthly paradise) and for restoration of our original relationship with the Creator.

But there is a cure. We may sometimes feel like the Israelites who hung their harps on the willows of Babylon and wept (Psalm. 137:2), but hope remains in God (Psalm. 42:11). God provides for us through the Earth, which remains His and which He still loves despite our sinful damage to it (Psalm. 24:1). While we may long for heaven and know that Christ has prepared a place there for us (John. 14:2), Revelation 21 shows us that, in the end, heaven will descend to Earth and all will be made new.

Week 2 /Day 4

BLACK DESERT

Speak to the people of Israel and say to them: When you enter the land that I am giving you, the land itself shall observe a Sabbath for the Lord. Leviticus 25:2

Driving through the cornfields of western Illinois in the summer reminds me of how seemingly productive and abundant the land is for these crops. A drive through the same area after harvest in winter reveals another picture—exposed black prairie soil from horizon to horizon. There is little protection or habitat for any species of bird or mammal as the wind blows across the expanse of barren soil.

Planting a monoculture of corn year after year leads to a depletion of soil nutrients and microorganisms. Artificial fertilizers then become necessary, and polluted surface runoff becomes a problem. As a result, some ecologists call this area a biological "black desert."

When the Lord instructed the Israelites how to care for their newly acquired land, He was very serious about not pushing the land's productivity too far. There was to be a year of rest every seven years. Apparently, this command was ignored. 2 Chronicles 36:21 states that because they ignored Sabbath rests (among other disobedience), the Israelites would spend 70 years in Babylon. During this time the land would get its rest.

There's a lesson in this for all of us caught up in the modern 24/7 mentality. "Rest" has become "recreation," which is often defined by physically stressful pursuits. Historically, Sunday was a day of rest, but now, for many people, Sunday is another day of activity. Mentally and physically, we need periods of rest. We need to rethink how God's wisdom concerning sufficient rest applies to our lives so we can make room for truly living. Otherwise, we risk having our spiritual and even our physical lives turned into a black desert.

Week 2 /Day 5

DEEP-ROOTED GRASSES IN CLUMPS OF CLAY

Because he cleaves to me in love, I will deliver him; I will protect him because he knows my name. Psalm 91:14 RSV

My community garden plot left a lot to be desired. Although it had been rototilled earlier in the spring, it was full of grass. It wasn't Bermuda grass, but it had the same growth characteristics—lots of underground stems (stolons), which, when cut or broken, resulted in even more grass. The only way to get rid of it was to dig deeply with a shovel and tease the tangled stolons and roots out of the soil. Although the grass was bothersome, it's tenacity and ability to survive impressed me.

I noticed that often the grass roots seemed to entwine around clumps of clay or more solid pieces of soil embedded within the generally sandy garden soil. These clumps of clay retain more moisture than the surrounding sandy soil, and evidently provide a more reliable source of water when the rest of the soil has dried out.

It made me wonder about us. What do we hold to in our lives? What sustains our lives when everything dries up around us? If it's simply the soil of this world, we will eventually shrivel and die along with it. But if we root on to Jesus, we will have access to peace in this world and eternal life in the next. Not a hard choice, is it?

This Coming Week

Observe a Sabbath Day by making rest and some prayer time a priority. This is a difficult assignment in our overly busy world.

Week 3 /Day 1

POLLINATORS

But the fruit of the Spirit is love, joy, peace, patience, kindness, generosity, faithfulness, gentleness, and self-control. Against such things there is no law. Galatians 5:22-23

It was always a springtime treat to pass a certain basswood or linden tree in bloom when I walked our dog around the neighborhood. Not only were the white flowers beautiful and fragrant, but the tree was literally alive with buzzing bees. I've not sampled any basswood honey, but I imagine it's wonderful. Besides their prolific honey production, bees are extremely valuable pollinators of many commercial crops.

One third of all our food grown in the US depends on pollinators—mostly honeybees and wild bees. Without these insects, we would have fewer apples, cherries, blueberries, almonds, and many other fruits and vegetables.

When we are baptized and receive Jesus into our lives, we begin blossoming as Christians. Then, as Jesus indicated to Nicodemus (John 3:1-5), when we truly confess our sin and acknowledge our total dependence on Jesus's justifying grace, we are "pollinated" and will begin bearing the fruits of the Spirit.

Week 3 /Day 2

TALKING TREES

You will go out in joy and be led forth in peace; the mountains and hills will burst into song before you, and all the trees of the field will clap their hands. Isaiah 55:12

We have vocal cords, a tongue, and a mouth that can form a kaleidoscope of sounds and speech as air is pushed out from our lungs. Trees have none of these things, yet they do have a repertoire of sound, thanks to the wind. Who hasn't heard the whispering of pines in the wind or the howl of winter gales through barren branches? Cottonwoods, quaking aspens, and similar trees have broad, flat leaves on long petioles (stems) that flap back and forth in even the slightest summer breezes. Isaiah may have had a similar tree species in mind when he wrote (55:12) that all the trees of the field would clap their hands in rejoicing at the return of Israel from Babylon.

Jesus appropriately compared the sound of the wind to the breath of the Holy Spirit in those who have been born again (John 3:8). The Hebrew word "ruach" and the Greek word "pneuma" are translated as "spirit" in Scripture. Both words have a basic meaning of "breath" or "wind."

Just as the Lord breathes life into us (Genesis 2:7), we need to breathe out praise to Him. Yet so many times we fail. As James (Chapter 3) clearly states, the tongue (and speech) is difficult to tame and can do great evil.

As the wind blows, trees have no choice as to the sounds they make. As we speak, we have a choice. Will it be uplifting, edifying, and in praise of the Lord, or will it be otherwise? If the Holy Spirit is blowing through our lives, the sounds of praise and promise will prevail.

LUCIFERIN, LUCIFERASE, AND LUCIFER

Watch out for false prophets. They come to you in sheep's clothing, but inwardly they are ferocious wolves. Matthew 7:15

Various species of fireflies put on their annual evening light show every June in our backyard. Near sunset, they start rising out of the grass and soon start flashing their lights as they fly through the air. Other fireflies begin flashing as they perch on grass blades, shrubs, or tree branches.

Fireflies are beetles, and they use their light-producing capabilities to communicate and find mates. The light they produce results from the breakdown of a pigment called luciferin in the presence of the enzyme luciferase. The frequency and pattern of flashes produced by each species of firefly is different, thus enabling males to find females of their species.

The females of certain firefly species are predaceous. They attract males of other species by mimicking their flashes. When the male lands, he is devoured by the female that tricked him.

Because of instinct, male fireflies don't exercise caution when it comes to responding to certain light flash patterns. We humans, however, have the capability of discerning the nature of what attracts us in this world. Satan (Lucifer) uses many attractions to lure us close enough to be devoured. We need to pray, stay in the Word, and be wary to avoid our spiritual destruction. We may consider ourselves superior to a male beetle in our discernment, but are we?

Week 3 /Day 4

NURSE PLANTS IN THE DESERT

The friend who attends the bridegroom waits and listens for him, and is full of joy when he hears the bridegroom's voice. That joy is mine, and it is now complete. He must become greater; I must become less. John 3:29-30

Creosote bush is a very tough plant found in Southwestern deserts. It's reportedly the most drought-resistant plant in North America and can go up to two years without rain. While hiking in the Superstition Mountains of Arizona, I noticed that small saguaro cacti often grew in the sparse shade of creosote bushes.

After a bit of research, I found that creosote bushes, palo-verde trees, mesquite trees, and other plants often shelter young saguaro cacti. These nurse plants offer protection from sun and frost until the cacti become better established in the desert environment. As the saguaros grow, their extensive root systems quickly absorb any rainfall and eventually contribute to the death of the nurse plant.

The botanical roles of nurse plants in the desert suggest the relationship of John the Baptist's ministry and the ministry of Jesus. John was the tough desert prophet preparing the way for Jesus's ministry. After baptizing Jesus, John stated that his ministry needed to decrease while Jesus's ministry was to increase (John 3:30).

As followers of Christ, we need this same attitude of humility demonstrated by John. Our role in ministry should not become one where we seek the spotlight or glory for ourselves. Rather we should always seek to decrease our visibility so that the glory goes to Christ. Likewise, in all our relationships as Christians, we need to seek ways of encouraging and helping others to grow as we decrease in our role as leader or mentor. (Philemon 2:3).

Week 3 /Day 5

PROTECTION

He who dwells in the shelter of the Most High will rest in the shadow of the Almighty. Psalm 91:1

As I looked out over the lake on a quiet spring morning, I noticed a single Ruddy Duck bobbing on the surface near the middle of the lake. Ruddy Ducks are small somewhat comical-looking diving ducks that migrate through our part of Michigan every spring. Suddenly the duck dove beneath the surface, and the shadow of low-flying Red-tailed Hawk passed over the water. A moment later, the Ruddy Duck reappeared safely on the surface. The water had provided protection from sudden danger.

Many passages of Scripture speak of God's protection. My favorite is Psalm 91, which I have prayed many times in seeking protection for myself and family members. There is but one requirement for God's protection and it is that we remain near to God through prayer, seeking to do His will.

Just as the duck was already in contact with the water surface and could easily dive beneath it for protection, so must Christians remain constantly in contact with the Lord if we seek His protection. Although we know that God does not intervene to prevent every physical or psychological injury in this life, He is always available to protect us from the greater threat of spiritual injury and death through sin. As James points out, "Come near to God, and He will come near to you" (James 4:8).

This Coming Week

Read an article about a current environmental issue such as climate change. Pray for discernment in how to live more lightly in God's beautiful garden.

Week 4 /Day 1

ASK THE PLANTS

But ask the animals, and they will teach you; the birds of the air, and they will tell you; ask the plants of the earth, and they will teach you, and the fish of the sea will declare to you. Job 12:7-8 (NRSV)

Dr. George Washington Carver, the son of a runaway slave, became a great biochemist. He is best known for research on the many uses of the peanut plant. His life and humble approach to science are outlined in the book *The Man Who Talks with the Flowers*.

Dr. Carver started every day of research with a walk outside, where he literally knelt down and spoke to the flowers. He then took care to listen to what they might be saying.

During the Renaissance, asking questions of God's creation is how modern science was birthed. The original quest of science was to find out more about the nature of God through discovery of nature's secrets. Of course, even the non-scientific among us can get some answers from plants just by observing them. Yellowing leaves usually mean a lack of certain nutrients in the soil or presence of disease. Wilting means insufficient water.

Psalm 19:1-4 states, "creation's voice goes out to all the Earth." Do we listen? We too often ignore what God is saying through creation (nature) at our own peril since we are totally dependent upon the provisions of the same. When glaciers disappear, species go extinct, sea birds die painfully covered in oil, and forests die—creation's voice is clear. If we do nothing, we are not living up to our God-given role as caring gardeners (Genesis 2:15).

Perhaps we don't always ask the plants because we don't want to hear God's answer through them—an answer demanding more humility, less greed, and more love for Him, each other, and His creation.

Week 4 /Day 2

THE SLANT OF LIGHT

Because of the Lord's great love we are not consumed, for his compassions never fail. They are new every morning; great is your faithfulness. Lamentations 3:22-23

Each morning I get up and do stretching exercises for the stenosis in my back. Since I do these exercises in the same room at the same time each day, it's easy to notice how the slant of morning sunlight through the window changes as the seasons progress. Most of us in the Northern Hemisphere start to notice shortening daylight hours by the end of August, but the change obviously begins immediately after summer solstice in June. Similarly, daylight starts lengthening each day following winter solstice in late December. Every day the beam of sunlight is new and different and arrives at a slightly different angle.

Sometimes it's hard to remember the newness and uniqueness of each day. Often it seems like the day will be the same old grind with the same repetitious tasks. Yet, every day the Lord gives us new grace and the possibility of seeing even the same old things in a new and more meaningful way. The Lord will never leave us nor forsake us even as the slant of time in our lives changes and we move closer to our own sunset.

Week 4 /Day 3

A PIECE OF THE ROCK

Look to the rock from which you were cut and to the quarry from which you were hewn. Isaiah 51:1

I enjoy walking the Lake Michigan beach near our home in western Michigan. I often pick up interesting small stones washed up by the lake's continual wave action. According to geologists, there are three main sources of these beach stones along Lake Michigan. These include igneous rocks like granite, quartz, agates, and basalt from the Canadian Shield; sedimentary rocks like limestone, dolomite, and sandstone from further north; and sedimentary rocks such as limestone and shale from bedrock around the southern portions of the lake.

While water and wind have scattered and mixed stones from all these sources over the eons, it's still possible to identify the original sources of these stones based on their physical characteristics.

As Christians, we are "stones" originating from Jesus, the "rock" of our salvation. To be recognized in this world as such, we need to maintain those unique spiritual qualities characteristic of our source. Paul lists these characteristics, as "fruits" of the spirit—love, joy, peace, forbearance, kindness, goodness, faithfulness, gentleness, and self-control. These traits in us testify to the world, the original "rock" to which we belong.

Week 4 /Day 4

ANCHOR

We have this hope as an anchor for the soul, firm and secure. It enters the inner sanctuary behind the curtain. Hebrews 6:19

My wife took the stern of the canoe and was going to paddle me around the lake as I fished for bluegills. Our canoe tends to drift easily on the water like a leaf. So, when a light breeze came up, my poor wife had to struggle to keep the canoe close to patches of lily pads and other potential fishing spots. Frustration reigned. After that outing, I decided it was time to buy a canoe anchor to help hold us in place, which made me think about the other anchors in my life.

It was the anchor and not the cross that was the earliest symbol among Christian believers. The anchor symbol was used extensively during the first 200–300 years of the Christian Church. It symbolized the belief that Christ would prevent the church from drifting away from faith during a time of persecution under the Romans.

Years ago, Ray Boltz sang a popular Christian song, "The Anchor Holds." The lyrics speak of a storm-battered ship of life with the sails torn, but the anchor holds. Tears come to my eyes whenever I hear that song. Our anchor in Christ will hold no matter how life or death pull at us. We are not dependent on ourselves or even on those around us for safety in the winds of life. Faith in Christ alone holds.

Week 4 /Day 5

WEEDER'S DILEMMA

I can do all things through Christ who strengthens me. Philippians 4:13

Through what seems like consistently poor planning on my part, my wife and I usually take a vacation during the peak summer growing season. This is a particularly bad time to leave my carefully tended garden. Other than receiving an occasional watering by a friend or neighbor, the garden is temporarily abandoned.

When I return from vacation, the garden is inevitably overgrown with weeds. I find myself staring at the weedy mess, wondering where, or if, to start weeding. Then Proverbs 24: 30-34 and the "field of the sluggard" comes to mind! At that point, I usually just concentrate on a small corner of the garden, bend down, and start pulling. Once a little progress is made, I become encouraged to press on.

This weeder's dilemma reminds me of what happens when we take a vacation from the Lord by sloughing off on our prayer life, getting out of the habit of weekly worship, letting our Bible collect dust. The weeds of life start sprouting up. To get back into spiritual discipline, we don't need to start big; we just need to start somewhere. With the help of the Holy Spirit, who strengthens us for the task (Philippians 4:13), we can regain the garden of faith, prayer by prayer.

This Coming Week

What have you been procrastinating about? Pray for the motivation to address whatever it is.

JULY DEVOTIONS

Contents

Week 1 /Day 1

ALLEGIANCE

Jesus said, "My kingdom is not of this world." John 18:36

Years ago, my wife and I attended an outdoor concert on a late summer evening. The concert was a memorial to those who lost their lives in the 9/11 attacks. The local symphony did a wonderful job playing various patriotic songs, and various fire and police personnel were recognized for their community service.

At one point in the concert, all were asked to stand for a moment of silence. We were near the edge of the seating area, and as we stood there, the crickets in the nearby shrubbery continued to chirp loudly. They seemed to be protesting our patriotism.

As Christians, we need to be careful not to over-extend our love of country to the point of turning it into an idol. Not that we shouldn't love our country, rejoice in its goodness, or mourn for our losses in peace and war, but we should also acknowledge that our first allegiance is to the Lamb.

The crickets were a reminder to me that God's concern, love, and mercy extend beyond all national and political borders—to all people. All kingdoms except the Kingdom of Heaven will eventually pass away.

Week 1 /Day 2

PROVISION

Look at the birds of the air; they do not sow or reap or store away in barns, and yet your heavenly Father feeds them. Matthew 6: 26-30

Jesus was a proponent of bird watching. The Gospels acknowledge that Jesus told His followers to "consider the birds of the air" (Matthew 6:26) and to "consider the ravens" (Luke 12:24). His analogy of birds was in the context of His followers not worrying about life. If God provides for lowly birds, why would He not provide for you?

I thought about God's provision for His creatures recently as I watched several Caspian terns around the lake near our home. Caspian terns are easily recognizable, with their dark heads and bright orange bills. These birds are beautiful in flight, but the most dramatic moment is when they see a fish near the surface and plunge-dive into the water from mid-air. This is a very different approach to the fishing technique that the great blue herons use. The herons stand motionless in the shallows, watching for fish, frogs, or other prey. Loons and cormorants use yet another approach. They swim on the surface in deeper water and then dive from the surface to catch fish.

Each bird is equipped with unique abilities and body structures to meet their daily food requirements. Yet they all depend on God's provision without worry. As Psalm 104:27 states, "These all look to you to give them their food at the proper time." Even though we sow, reap, and store food; humans are also ultimately dependent upon the hand of God for our daily provision. Our act of faith is to trust in the Lord in all things. If we do so, the Lord *will* provide. As Jesus said to His disciples, "Do not let your hearts be troubled, trust in God; trust also in me" (John 14:1).

Week 1 /Day 3

UNDERWINGS

Where then does wisdom come from: Where does understanding dwell? It is hidden from the eyes of every living thing, concealed even from the birds of the air. Job 28:20-21

A budding entomologist, I started an insect collection when I was a boy. I was especially interested in the showy butterflies—the monarchs and swallowtails. Moths weren't as exciting, until I discovered underwing moths. These are large moths usually found in wooded areas. At rest, their gray and brown forewings blend in perfectly with tree bark, which makes them difficult for birds to find. Yet if they are disturbed, they spread their wings, exposing colorful orange, black, pink, and red hind wings. Scientists think that sudden exposure of these colorful hind wings may startle or frighten away any birds that happen to find these moths.

Discovering the hidden beauty in nature—whether it's color hidden beneath moth wings, crystals formed inside a rocky geode, or a mathematically perfect explanation of some natural phenomenon— can be a metaphor for achieving wisdom. Knowledge and understanding are sometimes startling and cause us to see things in a totally different way.

Wisdom is not always like brightly colored butterflies that alight on your shoulder with no effort on your part. Instead, wisdom must often be sought out in our different life circumstances, which requires perseverance. If we, like Solomon, ask the Lord for wisdom in our daily life, we will eventually find it and possibly be changed by seeing our world and our lives in a radically different way.

Week 1 /Day 4

GOD'S PASTELS

But will God really dwell on Earth? The heavens, even the highest heaven, cannot contain you. How much less this temple I have built!
1 Kings 8:27

I remember attending a summer evening church service a couple of years ago. It was in a church where there was no view to the outside. Without natural light, the sanctuary was a little dark. The worship was excellent, and we prayed intensely for revival within the church and the community. We prayed with the expectancy that, in the phrase repeatedly used by the pastor, "God would show up."

As the service ended, I left the artificially lighted church interior to experience a gorgeous sunset of pastel colors painted across the western skies. While we were inside praying for God to show up, He was busy outside creatively—and maybe playfully—painting the sky.

How often do we miss His handiwork because we confine ourselves to temples of our own making? God cannot be contained in any special place in His creation. As the Lord states in Isaiah 66:1, "Heaven is my throne, and the Earth is my footstool. Where is the house you will build for me?" We should remain humbly mindful that God always shows up in the natural world He created if we but open our eyes. As David said in Psalm 19, "The heavens declare the glory of God; the skies proclaim the work of His hands." Remember to praise Him within the temple of His making—the whole universe.

Week 1 /Day 5

BEACH GRASS DIAMONDS

Let my teaching fall like rain and my words descend like dew, like showers on new grass, like abundant rain on tender plants. Deuteronomy 32:2

After a drizzly, gray day in early June, my wife and I decided to take a short walk on a nearby beach. Along the way, we found a large log and sat down to enjoy the early evening view. As the sun began to break out from behind the clouds, the raindrops reflecting off the beach grass appeared like hundreds of sparkling diamonds. While quite beautiful, "raindrop diamonds" are ephemeral. The sun or wind can quickly evaporate them, and they are gone. Real diamonds, on the other hand, as the commercial says, are forever. The hardest known substance on Earth, diamonds etymology is based on a Greek word for "unconquerable" or "indestructible."

Wouldn't it be wonderful if our own lives were like real diamonds, indestructible, rather than like those raindrop diamonds found on the beach? Our physical beings are ephemeral and fleeting, and this is pointed out numerous times in the Bible. Isaiah 40:6-7 states, "All people are like grass, and all their faithfulness is like the flowers of the field. The grass withers and the flowers fall." Psalm 90:5-6 also compares human life to grass: "people . . . are like the new grass of the morning . . . it springs up new, but by evening it is dry and withered." Or consider 2 Corinthians 4:18: "for the things which are seen are temporal, but the things which are not seen are eternal."

Life is short and soon we wither, but like grass we can catch the rain of Jesus' teaching of love and let it sparkle in His light. And if we are faithful to His word, at the end of our earthly life, we will be transformed from an ephemeral diamond into an eternal diamond, sparkling in God's never-ending glory.

This Coming Week

Pray Psalm 51:15 the first thing each morning. "Open my lips, Lord, and my mouth will declare your praise."

Week 2 /Day 1

COOLING DOWN

One who is slow to anger is better than the mighty, and one whose temper is controlled than the one who captures a city. Proverbs 16:32 NRSV

Radar showed strong storms moving northeast from northern Illinois and southern Wisconsin toward Lake Michigan. My wife and I lived in the storm's projected path on the opposite side of the lake. It looked like we could be in for gale force winds, pounding rain, and damaging hail.

Lake Michigan is a mighty body of water, and I was worried about what could happen as the storm gathered speed crossing it. To our surprise, by the time the storm arrived on our side, there was little more than some light rain and a gentle breeze. The cool lake waters stopped the rapid rise of hot humid air, which fueled the storms over land. As a result, the storms lost their punch.

Anger is often like an emotional storm, rising quickly and sometimes violently, threatening our emotional well-being. Like the hot air of a thunderstorm, blood rushes to our heads and our faces turn red. Angry words and actions may follow, causing us to say and do things we're most likely to regret later.

Many Proverbs in the Bible warn of uncontrolled anger: It's good sense to be slow to anger (Proverbs 19:11); anger breeds more strife (Proverbs 30:33); anger is folly (Proverbs 14:29; 29:11); and a gentle answer turns away wrath (Proverbs 15:1). Jesus reminds us in Matthew 5:22 that anger directed at others also subjects us to judgment.

Although I'm a long way from totally controlling anger in my own life, I pray for those fruits of the spirit—love, peace, patience, kindness, gentleness, and self-control—that can act as a cooling agent to defuse anger. With Christ's guidance I pray to work on this day by day, so that a reservoir of cooling waters is available when anger threatens to erupt.

Week 2 /Day 2

DEW-BAPTISED FEET

And how can they preach unless they are sent? As it is written, "How beautiful are the feet of those who bring good news!" Romans 10:15

Early morning walks in summer are great since you can just throw on some shorts, a t-shirt, and sandals and head out the door. Often, I get my feet wet walking through the dew-soaked grass. This experience makes me think of the importance of water as a symbol in Christian life—particularly baptism. Getting my feet wet on these early morning walks and quiet times with the Lord is, in a sense, like being baptized or rededicated to the Lord for the coming day.

Water in the form of dew was used by God as a symbol of promise to Gideon. Long before John the Baptist was baptizing in the Jordan, Gideon tested the will of God for his life by placing fleece on the ground and seeing where the dew would form (Judges. 6:36-38).

Getting our feet wet from time to time in the dewy grass can be a good reminder that the Lord promises to be with us day in and day out if we walk in His ways. It's a good reminder too that we are to take the Good News to others— "How beautiful are the feet of those who bring good news" (Isaiah 52:7-8).

Week 2 /Day 3

GORGEOUS HOLINESS

But just as He who called you is holy, so be holy in all you do; for it is written; "Be holy, because I am holy." 1 Peter 1:15

Cliffton Gorge State Nature Preserve in western Ohio is in a surprising place. You have no clue of its existence as you drive through the typical flat cornfields of western Ohio. Then, suddenly, you arrive at the edge of a 75-foot-deep tree-lined gorge cut through limestone bedrock by the Little Miami River.

The deep shade and cool spray from the river create an environment totally unique and vastly different from the surrounding cornfields. The plant community in the gorge contains many relict species that once were abundant as the last glaciers retreated from Ohio. These species have persisted for thousands of years in the protected cool, damp gorge. This is the reason the gorge has been set aside as a nature preserve.

Holiness means being set aside for God's purposes in the world. As Christians, we are called to be a holy people (Leviticus 11: 44-45, 19:2, 20:7 and 1 Peter 1:15-16). In a sense, then, the Christian community can be seen as a preserve of godliness in world that has largely forgotten God. The Christian mission is to ever-widen the boundaries of the preserve to draw more and more people to God's holiness and the peace and love that characterize it.

Week 2 /Day 4

LIGHTNING

He unleashes his lightning beneath the whole heaven and sends it to the ends of the earth. Job 37:3

We recently had an amazing thunderstorm, producing lightning that continually lit up the night sky and thunder that rolled unceasingly. The power released by such lightning is awesome, though also a little frightening. A tremendous amount of power is unleashed in a bolt of lightning. At the same time, there is something mild and nourishing associated with it.

Lightning breaks apart molecular nitrogen, which makes up almost 80 percent of our atmosphere. This atmospheric nitrogen is unavailable to plants. However, the lightning-modified nitrogen combines with oxygen and hydrogen in raindrops forming nitrates that plants need to grow.

God's lightning—His power and majesty displayed in the universe—is truly awesome. Think of exploding stars, black holes, comets, the roaring oceans, and so many other natural phenomena. But the wonderful news is that this same awesome God also encompasses all that is gentle, mild, loving, and life giving. He knows and loves each of us, and His Word, like a gentle rain, can nourish our lives if we are wise enough to let it soak into us.

Week 2 /Day 5

FRYING FISH

When they had gone ashore, they saw a charcoal fire there, with fish on it, and bread. Jesus said to them, "Bring some of the fish that you have just caught." John 21:9-10 NRSV

When my son was in Boy Scouts years ago, we went on a high adventure canoe/camping trip to the Boundary Waters of northern Minnesota. Despite mosquitoes, a couple of thunderstorms, and a lot of portaging, it was a wonderful time.

On the last day out, we went fishing off the island where we were camping. We caught a number of large bluegills, which we filleted, coated with batter, and fried over an open fire. As we sat there eating, darkness started to fall, and loons called in the distance. I felt enveloped in the experience of the North Woods, realizing that I would remember this moment my entire life. It was one of the outdoor moments where I most strongly felt the presence of the Lord.

In the passage from John 21, Jesus cooks breakfast for the disciples who had been out fishing. This is the point where, after eating, Jesus re-commissioned Peter (and the rest of the disciples) to feed His sheep. Just as Peter would never forget this encounter, which occurred during a fish and bread breakfast cooked on an open fire, we also need to remember that Peter's commission is also our commission as Christ-followers.

This Coming Week

Read Galatians 5:22-23 (Fruits of the Spirit). Also look up the key virtues, which include prudence, justice, fortitude, and temperance. Meditate on 1 Corinthians 13:13 (faith, hope, and love).

Week 3 /Day 1

QUIET DEPTHS

Deep calls to deep in the roar of your waterfalls; all your waves and breakers have swept over me. Psalm 42:7

Gale-force winds can whip up 12 to 15-foot waves when a storm rolls across Lake Michigan. The power of the breakers smashing into the rocks and crashing upon the beach is frightening, even from a distance.

Most of the lake will show unrest. The shallow areas near shore will churn and roil. The area just beyond will rise with white-capped rollers. Yet despite the surface mayhem, the deep waters offshore, where the lake bottom might reach a depth of 200 feet, remain calm.

All humans experience surface storms—events that deafen with a roar and threaten to wash everything out of the way. These are times when deep faith in God and connection with His Holy Spirit can provide the peace that surpasses all understanding. Through faith, there is an ability to connect in the depth of our souls with the deep mysteries of God's love. Inside those depths it is possible to find quiet and rest, despite the storms of life.

Week 3 /Day 2

FINDING A GOOD GUIDE

I know every bird in the mountains, and the insects in the fields are mine. Psalm 50:11

As someone who enjoys the outdoors—particularly birding and fishing—I have come to appreciate guides who know the local territory, understand the habits of the animals I am seeking, and can take me where they are located. I am not alone. People pay substantial amounts of money for charter fishing boats, big game hunting guides, guides for birding in exotic locations, or climbing guides to lead the way up a challenging mountain.

If we find a good guide and are successful in catching fish, or bagging game, or sighting birds, or standing on the peak, we rejoice—much in the way of the widow in Luke 15:8-10 who swept her house and found her lost coin. Like the woman in the story, our joy often comes in sharing our fishing and hunting stories, our birding adventures, and climbing accomplishments with friends.

Our spiritual life can also be an adventure to share. Just as we gather information to read about our intended trip, we can read about the adventures of others in the Bible. We then listen closely and follow our Guide in prayer. After experiencing the excitement of whatever quest, we follow, we will have stories to share with others that may motivate them to embark on their own adventures with Jesus—the best Guide in the universe.

Week 3 /Day 3

GARDEN SACRAMENTS

I will send down showers in season; there will be showers of blessing. The trees of the field will yield their fruit and the ground will yield its crops; the people will be secure in their land. Ezekiel 34:26-27

Every summer I look forward to the day when I can pick the first juicy, red ripe tomato off the vine in the garden. It's a "sacramental" moment for me when I bite into that tomato still warm from the morning sun, and the full flavor of that vine-ripened fruit bursts in my mouth. While theologically this annual ritual may not be recognized as a sacrament, it nevertheless brings thankfulness to God from my heart for His provision, which is close enough for me.

"Sacrament" is defined as "a formal religious ceremony conferring a specific grace on those who receive it." "Grace" is "an unearned/undeserved blessing of God's love, which could involve creation, life, or salvation." My little tomato ritual isn't very formal, but it certainly confers a specific grace on me. It focuses my thoughts on the miracle of plant growth that takes God's provisions of soil, nutrients, water, sun, carbon dioxide and oxygen to produce a tasty fruit.

The Lord promised Ezekiel that He would send down showers of blessings (Ezekiel 34:26). Only when we slowdown from our busyness and open our eyes to even the smallest of sacramental moments can we experience the blessings God has for us.

Week 3 /Day 4

STRATIFIED

May the God of hope fill you with all joy and peace, as you trust in Him, so that you may overflow with hope by the power of the Holy Spirit. Romans 15:13

During summers in temperate regions across North America, deeper lakes stratify. Sunlight penetrates and warms the upper layers of water where plant growth occurs, and there is plenty of oxygen for fish and other organisms. The lower cold-water layer lies deeper, where little sunlight penetrates. This lower cold, dark layer has little oxygen and little life, but nutrients accumulate in the bottom sediment. In the fall, lake waters cool, and wind stirs the water. The stratified layers mix, making all the water the same temperature and moving bottom nutrients throughout the entire lake to the benefit of all life in the lake.

Our lives are sometimes stratified like a lake in summer. We only use the easier-to-reach part of our potential in living a life for Christ. We hold back from getting involved or from using our talents in ways that could further the Kingdom.

If your life is stratified, pray for the Holy Spirit to stir the waters and bring new enthusiasm, energy, and creativity to your Christian life. Paul exhorted us in Romans 12:1-2 to present our bodies as a living sacrifice, which is our reasonable service to God. The Lord wants all of us, not just a part. Stepping out in faith, you may find that you have a lot more potential in many more areas than you ever imagined.

BETWEEN WORLDS

My prayer is not that you take them out of the world but that you protect them from the evil one. John 17:15

Water striders are insects that effortlessly skate around on quiet water surfaces of ponds and lakes in search of food and mates. Research has shown that water striders have minute setae (hairs) on their feet that trap tiny air bubbles. The combination of these tiny air bubbles and water's natural surface tension allows water striders to live in their very unusual habitat—the surface between the aquatic world and the air. Living between these two worlds has dangers from both below and above. Fish may come to the surface to devour them, or a dragonfly may swoop down from above for a meal.

Much like water striders, Christians also live between worlds. We are told to be *in* the world, but not *of* it (John 17:14-15). We are also instructed to be the hands and feet of Christ bringing Good News to a hurting world (1 Corinthians 12:27). Negotiating our way between this world and the Kingdom of Heaven has its dangers. We can easily be devoured from below by sin, or we can become as the cliché goes, "so heavenly minded, we're of no earthly good." We must walk the line of not falling into the ways of the world but also not isolating ourselves from the world and thus losing our influence to further the Gospel.

It's only through the spiritual disciplines of prayer, fasting, and daily self-examination that we can, with God's help, be transformed (Romans 12:1-2) and live successfully as Christians while navigating the tension between two worlds.

This Coming Week

Listen this week for the Lord calling out to you to leave your comfort zone and step out in faith. Look at the needs around you and evaluate the gifts you have that the Lord might use to help others.

Week 4 /Day 1

VIRGA

As the rain and snow come down from heaven, and do not return to it without watering the earth and making it bud and flourish, so that it yields seed for the sower and bread for the eater, so my word that goes out from my mouth: It will not return to me empty. Isaiah 55:10-11

Cumulus clouds bubbled up over the desert mountains as morning progressed toward noon. Gray streaks of rain appeared beneath some of the larger clouds. These filmy gray curtains faded as they extended earthward, disappearing into nothingness in the desert sky, no moisture reached the thirsty desert soil. This meteorological phenomenon is called "virga," and it occurs when rain falls into very dry air and evaporates before reaching the surface of the Earth.

In order to water the Earth—to be life giving—rain must obviously reach the ground. In the same manner, for God's Word to reach people—to be life giving—the Word has to reach them. If the Good News doesn't touch down and contact others, it will have no effect. Making contact is vital and bringing the Word into the world isn't up to just missionaries and full-time evangelists. It's up to each one of us.

God has promised that once His Word reaches people, it will accomplish its purpose in their lives. Let's resolve to bring the rain of God's love and mercy into the lives of everyone we encounter.

Week 4 /Day 2

CLOUD SHADOW

As heat is reduced by the shadow of a cloud, so the song of the ruthless is stilled. Isaiah 25:5

The sun blazed down in the still, hot air as I worked in the garden. The high humidity made the heat even more oppressive. Unexpectedly, the intensity of the heat waned slightly for a few moments as a tiny cloud passed overhead. A barely discernable breeze accompanied the cloud's shadow.

Sometimes the difficulties and trials in our lives seem as unrelenting as the hot blazing sun of a midsummer heat wave. During these times, we may wonder why God allows bad things to happen. David asked this same question in Psalm 22, the words of which were repeated by Jesus on the cross: "My God, my God, why have you forsaken me?"

Although resolution and relief from certain trials we experience may be long in coming or may never come in this life, some level of respite will occur as we hold on to our faith in Christ. The shadow of His protecting wings—like a small cloud—can give us hope to carry on regardless of ongoing difficulties.

Week 4 /Day 3

THE LAND MOURNS

Therefore the land mourns, and all who live in it languish; together with the wild animals and the birds of the air, even the fish of the sea are perishing. Hosea 4:3 ESV

Although some still deny it, the scientists who have been predicting climate change for decades are proven more and more correct by the day. Each more powerful storm, receding glacier, bleached coral reef, and rise in sea level confirms dire predictions.

Christians are no less part of the moral problem behind climate change. We are not caring for the garden (Genesis 2:15) as God charged us. Instead, we prefer to enjoy our lifestyles that through their dependence on carbon-based fuels are potentially wrecking the future habitability of Earth for our children's children.

In Hosea, the land mourns as a result of the moral bankruptcy of the people and their turning from God. Today, as a result of generations of selfishness and international as well as national injustices, the entire Earth has entered mourning through climate change.

Paul writes in Galatians 6:7: "God is not mocked, for you reap what you sow." We too have turned from God and are rapidly turning His beautiful creation of Earth into an unsustainable hell. It is time for all of us, Christians included, to make the changes we are called upon to make as the creation waits in eager expectation for the children of God to be revealed (Romans 8:19).

Week 4 /Day 4

FATA MORGANA

Do not love the world or the things in the world. The love of the Father is not in those who love the world; for all that is in the world—the desire of the flesh, the desire of the eyes, the pride in riches—comes not from the Father but from the world. 1 John 2:15-16

One cool summer evening my wife and I were walking along the Lake Michigan beach near our house. As we looked out across the lake through the gathering darkness my wife said she saw what appeared to be lights from the skyline of Milwaukee more than 80 miles away. As I stared into the distance, I saw something that looked like lighted buildings on the horizon. Another couple we passed on the beach also said they saw the lights. They said this was a meteorological phenomenon that appeared on rare occasions along the eastern Lake Michigan shoreline. With a little research I found out that the mirage we had seen was called *fata morgana.*

There needs to be a stable warm air layer above cooler surface air for a fata morgana to develop. The layer of warm air refracts the light from the actual object (in this case the Milwaukee skyline) and bends it down at angles that can be quite distant from the source. There have been reports over the centuries of all kinds of fata morgana involving sailors seeing phantom ships such as the famous Flying Dutchman. Such mirages have even resulted in shipwrecks.

This business of mirages made me think of how we live in a commercial world of mirages, those often-distant enticing things of the world—status, beauty, power, and wealth. These things can easily confuse our spiritual navigation towards a Christ-like life. Grasping for any of these mirages can leave us spiritually shipwrecked. Jesus guides us to pursue the real things of eternal value. As the question is asked in Matthew 16:26, what will it profit someone to gain the whole world but lose their soul?

Week 4 /Day 5

THE BALM IN GILEAD

Is there no balm in Gilead? Is there no physician there? Why then has the health of my poor people not been restored? Jeremiah.8: 22 NRSV

There is a plant related to *Commiphora gileadensis* that grows in the mountains east of the Jordan River. These plants were probably the source of the healing balm mentioned several times in the Bible.

In our modern world, half of all pharmaceuticals in use originated—or are still made from—chemicals isolated from plants. Scientists continue bioprospecting for promising plants throughout the world.

But Jeremiah wasn't talking about needing a headache cure for the Israelites. He was talking about a cure that somehow could restore a people's faith in God.

I realize every day the need for the Great Physician to heal my "sin-sick soul" (as the old gospel song says). I need an astringent to dry up my addiction to status and things, a soothing ointment to heal and anointing oil to strengthen. There is a balm in Gilead—His name is Jesus.

This Coming Week

Check for new and creative ways to strengthen your prayer life. Examples might be to go on a prayer walk, do a partial fast, light a candle when you begin to pray, chose a special room or place at home for prayer.

AUGUST DEVOTIONS

Contents

Week 1 /Day 1

PINE PRAISES

Like a cedar of Lebanon he will send down his roots; his young shoots will grow. His splendor will be like an olive tree, his fragrance like a cedar of Lebanon. Hosea 14:5-7

I always enjoyed a morning walk with the family dog, using the opportunity to spend quiet time with the Lord. Among the many trees along the streets of our neighborhood, one Scotch pine tree is a particular favorite of mine.

On calm, warm mornings, the tree filled the air with wonderful pine fragrance; and in the spring of each year, the tree candled with new needle growth at the tip of each branch. This tree always reminded me how nature itself praises the Lord for all that it has been given. Fragrance of pine is incense in praise to the Lord. The candles of new growth form prayers of thanksgiving for the promise of spring and the Resurrection.

The tree, as with all non-human creation, had no choice but to praise and reflect its Creator with all its life. As God's children, we do get to make choices. How faithful are we in making our lives a pleasing aroma to the Lord? Are our lives candles of light to those around us? Perhaps we should take a lesson from the lowly pine tree and offer our lives as praise for the Lord!

Week 1 /Day 2

OUT OF THE DARKNESS

For you were once in darkness, but now you are light in the Lord.
Ephesians 5:8

Cicadas are just one group of insect species, commonly recognized in the Midwest by their familiar droning in the treetops during hot summer afternoons and evenings. Few of us, however, give much thought to the rest of the story about cicadas, and most of that story takes place underground.

After female cicadas lay their eggs in the tips of tree branches, the newly emerged nymphs drop to the ground and head for underground tree roots to feed. Annual cicada nymphs spend most of one year underground before emerging. Periodic cicada nymphs may remain underground for 13 to 17 years. Once they do emerge, they undergo one more change.

I often find the cast "skins" of cicada nymphs at the base of tree trunks in late spring and early summer. These are the remains of a transition from the dark underground, flightless life of a nymphal cicada to the bright aboveground free-flying life of an adult. They remind me of the changes that occur in our spiritual lives between the time we "walk in darkness" and the time we accept the Good News of Christ. Just as cicadas have winged freedom once they become airborne adults, we have new freedom once we have accepted Jesus Christ.

Week 1 /Day 3

SPROUTING THROUGH THE CRACKS

"My thoughts are not your thoughts, nor are your ways my ways,"
says the Lord." For as the heavens are higher than the earth, so are
my ways higher than your ways, and my thoughts than your
thoughts." Isaiah 55:8-9

Ailanthus—also known as Tree of Heaven—is native to China,
brought to the U.S. in the late 1700s. The tree is now common
throughout most of the country. It can survive and thrive in poor
soils and in urban environments where few other trees can grow.
Ailanthus often grows in tight clusters since suckers sprout from the
spreading roots making the tree invasive and difficult to kill. It has
large compound leaves and blooms early to mid-summer. Although
the flower clusters are attractive to look at, they smell like rotting
peanuts.

Walk through many urban neighborhoods, and you will see a Tree of
Heaven poking through a sidewalk crack, growing along the fence of
a parking lot, or sprouting up along the side of an abandoned
building. The uninviting places where this tree can grow and even
provide beauty and shade are a reminder that heaven can break
through in the most unlikely places.

Just as we can find fault with many of this tree's horticultural
characteristics, so we often find fault with God's ways in our lives.
We may be praying for an oak but get a Tree of Heaven in our life
circumstances. When this happens, we need to remind ourselves that
God's ways are not our ways, and His thoughts are not our thoughts.
With the help of the Holy Spirit, we can find ways of appreciating the
Trees of Heaven in our lives (or even being a Tree of Heaven
ourselves) remembering that with the help of the Holy Spirit, we can
bloom and thrive wherever we sprout in God's Kingdom.

Week 1 /Day 4

THUNDERSTORM CHANGES

Jesus answered, "I tell you the truth, no one can enter the kingdom of God unless he is born of water and the Spirit." John 3:5 NRSV

Thunderstorms are frequent during Midwest summers. They often precede cold fronts moving from the north and west into hot humid air coming up from the Gulf of Mexico. The colder air wedges under the warm humid air pushing it up and causing moisture to condense, forming rain. Once a thunderstorm is underway, cold air rushes out in front as the storm moves across the landscape.

The sequence of events associated with an approaching and passing thunderstorm—wind, rain, air mass change—remind me of the experience of being born again. The wind of the Holy Spirit may seem cold at first, unsettling our spiritual lives, yet making us aware that change is possible. The water of baptism (rain) is then a sign that we are ready to commit to a life in the Spirit. Finally, an atmospheric change occurs in our lives as we are bathed in the calm coolness of a life transformed for Christ.

The next time you experience a thunderstorm, thank the Lord for the atmospheric changes available to anyone baptized of water and spirit.

Week 1 /Day 5

TAKE OFF THE OLD COAT

Rather, clothe yourselves with the Lord Jesus Christ, and do not think about how to gratify the desires of the sinful nature. Romans 13:14

I enjoy folk or bluegrass style gospel music. The earthiness and simple honesty of these songs can be a powerful testimony to God's love for us and for the hope we have in Christ. One song I particularly like by Patty Loveless is "Two Coats." The song refers to taking off the tattered and torn old coat of sin and replacing it with the new coat of a life in Jesus. In the Bible, Paul refers to a similar idea, putting aside the deeds of darkness and putting on the armor of light (Romans 13:12).

Many animals—such as insects, snakes, lobsters, and spiders—must regularly shed their exterior coverings in order to grow. Some plants also shed their old coats.

Sycamore trees litter the ground around them every summer as they shed thin pieces of exterior bark to allow for growth.

What a great reminder to us as Christians that we must take off our own old coats and clothe ourselves in the light of the Holy Spirit repeatedly throughout our lives as we continue to grow in the love of Jesus.

This Coming Week

Spend some time this week thinking about the obstacles in your life that may be robbing you of joy and peace. Ask the Lord to help you gain freedom from these hindrances.

Week 2 /Day 1

AMONG THE WALKING WOUNDED

For all have sinned and fall short of the glory of God. Romans 3:23

Aldo Leopold was a famous conservationist of the last century most known for his book *Sand County Almanac.* In his book, he attempted to show people that land is not just a commodity to be used and discarded. Many of the Old Testament prophets also warned the Israelites of dire consequences if they did not care for the land the way God intended. The heart of both these messages was to get people to see the land with new eyes of respect and responsibility.

"One of the penalties of an ecological education," writes Leopold, "is that one lives in a world of wounds." Christians particularly should be aware that we live in a world wounded in many ways by sinful behavior and that environmental degradation and social injustice are moral issues.

Our sins of selfishness and greed harm not only the Earth but also our brothers and sisters with whom we share the planet. As Christians we need to face the consequences of our sins against God's creation. We need to pray for the strength to make changes in our own lives and to make others aware that all of our wounded souls need treatment with wisdom from the Lord.

Week 2 /Day 2

CHRISTIAN EVAPORATION

So neither he who plants nor he who waters is anything, but only God, who makes things grow. 1 Corinthians 3:7

It was a long summer dry spell, but the afternoon sky looked ominous, and the smell of rain was in the air. A few drops started hitting the pavement here and there. It was one of those "three-inch" rains—three inches between raindrops. Soon even this little rain stopped, and you could see the water evaporating off of the hot pavement. It seemed that those few drops did nothing but help raise the humidity. Later that day, however, we had a significant rainfall.

At times, my Christian journey feels like one of those three-inch rains falling on hot pavement—sort of a spiritual evaporation, a feeling that I do little to alleviate the world's physical and spiritual thirst. Then I think of Paul's analogies to us all being part of the Body of Christ (1 Corinthians 12:27-30). He reminds us that some are called to do the planting, some the watering, and some the harvesting (1 Corinthians 3:6-9). Maybe my job for now is just to raise the humidity!

Week 2 /Day 3

BEAUTIFUL FEET

Now that I, your Lord and Teacher, have washed your feet, you also should wash one another's feet. John 13:14

The human foot is a beautiful creation. Each foot contains 26 separate bones; 33 joints; and over 100 muscles, tendons, and ligaments which all work in synchrony to provide balance and mobility. We often take our feet for granted—until something goes wrong. Then we may become painfully aware of how important our feet are in our daily lives.

As stated in Isaiah 52:7 and reiterated by Paul in Romans 10:15, "How beautiful are the feet of those who bring good news." No matter how dirty or smelly, if our feet carry us through life sharing the Good News, they are beautiful and holy. When Jesus washed the apostles' feet at the Last Supper, I wonder whether He thought of the fulfillment of God's promise through each beautiful foot He washed. Empowered by the Holy Spirit, those dirty feet would soon be carrying the Gospel throughout the world.

Week 2 / Day 4

SHAPED BY THE WIND AND SPIRIT

The wind blows wherever it pleases. You hear its sound, but you cannot tell where it comes from or where it is going. So it is with everyone born of the Spirit. John 3:8

While driving across the Southwest, my wife and I stopped at Painted Desert National Park in northern Arizona. The landscape of the park is barren, and the few scattered trees and shrubs surviving in this harsh environment are sculpted by the wind. The branches are shorter on the prevailing windward side and longer on the leeward side. The invisible hand of the wind is made visible in the growth habit of the trees or shrubs.

Jesus uses the wind as a metaphor for the Spirit in His conversation with Nicodemus (John 3:8). The wind of the Holy Spirit ushered in a highly visible change in the apostles and led to the beginnings of the Church. It continues to blow through the lives of Christian believers today, manifesting itself in the visible growth of the Spirit (Galatians 5:22-23).

Of all creatures created by God, Christians are the most capable of making visible the love of the invisible Spirit of God. It's by allowing the constant wind of the Spirit into our lives that we can be formed, shaped, and transformed to reflect His love.

Week 2 /Day 5

MAGNIFIED

And Mary said, "My soul doth magnify the Lord." Luke 1:46 KJV

I'm a casual bird watcher and especially enjoy watching how the birdlife during migration changes on the little lake near our Michigan condo. We can see across the lake from our balcony, and usually keep a pair of binoculars in a convenient kitchen drawer.

One day while rummaging through our storage room, I found an old pair of binoculars that were more powerful than the binoculars we had been using. The first time my wife used the newly found binoculars to scan the lake, she claimed she saw a loon. This sighting was very unusual for such a small, shallow lake. We checked the field guide; we both looked at the bird through the higher-powered binoculars and checked the field guide again. It was, indeed, a loon— the first one we had ever seen on the lake. The stronger magnification of those binoculars really helped!

Our Christian calling asks us to magnify Jesus for the world to see more clearly. This is essentially a counter-cultural calling. We magnify what we believe in by how we live, and it's important to evaluate exactly what that means. Are we magnifying ourselves, our possessions, and our power? Or are we magnifying Christ working in the world? A Christian life can indeed be a "pair of binoculars" for others to see the Lord more clearly, but we need to make sure we're focused on Him or we may lead others to a misidentification.

This Coming Week

Take off your shoes and walk in the grass. Think about how separated we are in our daily lives from the natural world.

Week 3 /Day 1

RUNNING (OR SWIMMING) AHEAD

Humble yourselves, therefore, under God's mighty hand, that He may lift you up in due time. 1Peter 5:6 NRSV

A pair of mute swans nested near our condo this spring, and now six cygnets follow their mother around the lake learning how to be swans. The father stays to the rear of these flotillas, watching for any danger from behind. The cygnets usually stay very close behind their mother, but occasionally, they will paddle hard and move out in front. When this happens, she immediately moves to get back in front of them. She knows the danger of small swans swimming on the lake by themselves.

I too tend to move out ahead of the Lord in my impatience to grow as a Christian. But to separate ourselves from God's timing and guidance in our lives is not a good plan. Such impatience can make us vulnerable to spiritual and, sometimes, to physical danger. Consider how Abraham "moved ahead of the Lord" in his relationship with Hagar (Genesis 16:1-5), or how Israel often moved ahead of the Lord in its dealings with surrounding enemy nations (Isaiah 30:1-2).

The advice of the psalmist in Psalm 130:5 is that we must wait on the Lord, in His Word. Only through the discipline of patience and by letting the Lord lead will we remain safe in His love.

Week 3 /Day 2

SYMMETRY

Who has measured the waters in the hollow of his hand, or with the breadth of his hand marked off the heavens? Who has held the dust of the earth in a basket or weighed the mountains on the scales and the hills in a balance? Isaiah 40:12

I've often looked at flowers, sunsets, or mountains, and wondered why we consider these aspects of creation beautiful. Unlike certain styles of dress, body makeup, or even music—where beauty is often contested—people from many different cultures call these natural objects and phenomena *beautiful*.

The concept of beauty is often associated with order, balance, and symmetry. Symmetry is found in mathematics, physical laws, molecules, and biological systems. Animals can be asymmetrical (no symmetry) like an amoeba or a sponge, radially symmetrical (circularly organized) like a jellyfish or a sand dollar, or bilaterally symmetrical (a definite right and left side) like most animals, including humans. All of which are considered beautiful.

God's creative handprint of beauty is evident throughout nature, yet when it comes to how God views us, His children, external appearance and symmetry are not important. Rather, symmetry is reflected internally, in the fruits of the Spirit. A spiritual symmetry of love, joy peace, patience, kindness, goodness, faithfulness, gentleness, and self-control is the basis of soul beauty. And the really good news is that, unlike external beauty, internal beauty based on this kind of symmetry never has to fade with age.

Week 3 /Day 3

CHICORY

Be joyful always, pray continually, give thanks in all circumstances, for this is God's will for you in Christ Jesus.
1 Thessalonians 5:16

Chicory is a blue-flowered weed often lining Midwest highways in mid- to late summer. It doesn't seem to mind the lousy roadside growing conditions. Poor dry soil, road salt residue, and oily runoff doesn't seem to faze it. It gathers moisture from very deep taproots.

Not only has chicory developed special adaptations that allow it to tolerate high levels of salt in soils, but the weed is a boon to humans as well. Chicory leaves are nutritious for people and livestock, and the roots can be roasted to make a coffee-like beverage.

Sometimes along life's roadway God plants us in tough situations—family problems, loneliness, sickness, and loss—making our spiritual growth a challenge. Let's face it, at times it's difficult to follow Paul's advice and "rejoice and give thanks in all circumstances" (1 Thessalonians 5:16-24).

During such difficult times, we need to develop deep taproots of prayer to reach into the healing waters of the Holy Spirit. With an abiding trust in the Lord through prayer, we will gain nourishment and the ability to withstand the "pollutants" surrounding our situation. The situation may not change, but through God's grace we will not only survive, but we will bloom like the chicory and be able to share our nourishment with others around us.

Week 3 /Day 4

DROUGHT

He will be like a tree planted by the water that sends out its roots by the stream. It does not fear when heat comes; its leaves are always green. It has no worries in a year of drought and never fails to bear fruit. Jeremiah 17:8

Hurricanes, tornadoes, and floods often grab the headlines for the sudden weather-related disasters they cause, but drought is often much more devastating. Crops wither, grass turns brown and breaks off underfoot, dust storms rage, rivers and streams and wells go dry. Animals die in great numbers when unable to find water. The destruction caused by a drought is insidiously slow, which is why it often doesn't make the headlines until after much of the damage has already occurred.

Drought was often used to accomplish God's purposes in the Old Testament. Famine and drought created the circumstances for reconciliation between Joseph and his brothers, and reunited Joseph with his father Jacob (Genesis 42 - 50). God confirmed Elijah as his prophet by means of drought (1 Kings 17:1). Jeremiah prophesized drought as punishment against the Babylonians for their capture and treatment of the Israelites (Jeremiah 50:38), and the Israelites were encouraged to start rebuilding the temple under the threat of drought (Haggai 1:11).

Spiritual drought happens to the most committed Christians. Even Mother Teresa reported that she felt spiritually dry throughout most of her life. Yet, she remained faithful to God's calling. We also need to recognize that this may be God's way of making us move beyond where we've been in our faith. When you feel spiritually parched, continue on in prayer, study the Word, and wait on the Lord. In other words, sink your roots of faith even deeper. Mercy and grace will once again rain down on your faithfulness.

Week 3 /Day 5

DUST DEVILS

Fear of the Lord is the beginning of knowledge. Proverbs 1:7

Dust devils, with their columns of swirling dust and debris, are common sights in the western high plains and deserts. These whirlwinds form when a pocket of hot air near the surface rises quickly through cooler air and begins to rotate. Dust devils are most common in hot weather and under sunny skies. They are not usually strong enough to do much damage, but if you are caught in one, it gets your attention with swirling dust that gets in your eyes and nose and can blow off your hat.

God often makes the winds His messengers (Psalm104: 4). God spoke to Job out of a whirlwind as He questioned Job's understanding (Job 38:1). The prophet Nahum warned the people of Nineveh that God's way was in the whirlwind and the storm (Nahum 1:3).

The Lord often allows whirlwinds—minor illnesses, disappointments, and misunderstandings—in our lives. Maybe they aren't tornados in their destructive power, but they get your attention. When this happens, we need to remember what little we understand of the true nature and power of God. He said to Job, "Who is this that darkens my counsel with words without knowledge?" This is the same God who the psalmist heard in the thunder and whirlwind—the Lord God Almighty is His name (Psalm 77:18; Jeremiah 50:34; Revelation 11:17).

While many Christians say they look forward to the coming of Christ, we're talking about the God of the universe. Let's not pretend we are righteous enough to stand tall in the whirlwind of His presence.

This Coming Week

Read Job 38:1-7 and consider how little we still understand of God's universe despite our scientific advances.

Week 4 /Day 1

CONDORS AND DARK ANGELS

And I saw an angel standing in the sun, who cried in a loud voice to all the birds flying in midair, "Come gather together for the great supper of God." Revelation 19:17

On a field trip several years ago, I watched several condors gliding above the mountains of northern Arizona. Unlike the much more common turkey vulture with a wingspan of 6 feet, condors glide effortlessly on 9-foot wingspans. Their sharp eyes scan the rugged desert floor for carcasses. Condors and other vultures seem to be dark angels charged with the unpleasant but necessary task of cleaning up the dead from the landscape.

As God's messengers, angels often are portrayed in Scripture as bearers of good news and help. Yet there are some passages where angels are darker messengers associated with death and destruction on behalf of God's justice. Consider the angel in 2 Samuel 24:16 who had intended to destroy Jerusalem, or in 2 Kings 19:35, when the angel of the Lord went out and put to death a hundred and eighty-five thousand in the Assyrian camp.

It's hard to read some of these accounts of God's justice meted out through the agency of angels because as much as time changes, some things remain the same. Innocent people often suffer and die because of the sins of their leaders. The injustices and inequities of national governments and international finance result in daily suffering and death. We follow "a way that appears to be right, but in the end leads to death." Proverbs 14:12

By building a world of inequity among peoples and nations, we have invited dark angels into the world. Pray for God's mercy and forgiveness for this transgression and remember that eventually God's justice and love will prevail.

Week 4 /Day 2

BLACK HILLS HAIL

I lift my eyes to the hills—where does my help come from? My help comes from the Lord, the Maker of heaven and Earth. Psalm 121:1-2

As my wife and I drove through the high plains of Wyoming, the sun burned down, and a hot dry wind blew across the grasslands. You could almost feel yourself dehydrating in the heat and low humidity.

At mid-afternoon we noticed thunderheads building in the far distance toward the Black Hills of South Dakota—our destination for the night. By late afternoon, we were on the road ascending out of the plains and into the Black Hills. As the dry grasslands gave way to open ponderosa pine forests, we were suddenly surrounded by hail-covered ground left by a recent passing thunderstorm. A faint, cool mist rose over the ground and into the green pine boughs—a picture of wonderful refreshment after the unrelenting heat of the plains.

Speaking to Isaiah in a dream, the Lord promised refreshment to His people weary of their long captivity (Isaiah 31:25). The same is offered to us. At times we may feel like captives in the dry hot plains of loss, fatigue, depression, or sickness; but the Lord offers us spiritual refreshment if we just ask Him. Take a few minutes throughout the day and go to the mountain of God for refreshment. Then try to find a longer time each day in your schedule to rest silently in the cool shade of God's presence. You don't even need to actively pray when you visit the mountain. The Lord will know you are there. Just go, let Him refresh you in love.

Week 4 /Day 3

TWISTED TRUNKS

Sing for joy, O heavens, for the Lord has done this; shout aloud, O Earth beneath. Burst into song, you mountains, you forests and all your trees, for the Lord has redeemed Jacob, He displays his glory in Israel. Isaiah 44:23

The gnarled trunk of a wind-twisted juniper pointed its bony finger toward the cobalt blue sky. Despite the harsh environment at the rim of the Grand Canyon, the juniper grew. It had long provided blessings in the form of food for wildlife, shelter for birds, and shade from the sun. The wizened tree, rooted into rock crevices and exposed to a lifetime of wind and storms, had finally succumbed. Yet its toughened trunk remained a testament to the tree's persistence and years of survival under the harshest of growing conditions.

Early in his life, Solomon was not only wise in governance, he was also a naturalist: teaching about the cedars of Lebanon, about hyssop that grows out of walls, and about many animals, including, birds, reptiles, and fish (1 Kings 4:33). He later used wood from the cedars of Lebanon to construct the temple for God's glory. Although in his old age Solomon turned from God and lost God's favor (1 Kings 11), his temple remained long after his death as a testament to his original faithfulness.

God promises in Psalm 92:12 and in Isaiah 65:22 that his people will flourish like a tree if they remain righteous. But the only way we will leave any testament to a righteous life rooted in God is through our reliance on Jesus. As Paul states in Romans 3:9-18, no one is righteous of their own accord. Let's resolve not to drift away from the Lord as we age, but to be persistent and stand as a testament to the promises of Christ.

Week 4 /Day 4

HO-HUM

Be joyful always; pray continually; give thanks in all circumstances, for this is God's will for you in Jesus Christ. 1 Thessalonians 5:17

Driving into an area where ecosystems change from one to another always fascinates me. I remember as a kid traveling with my parents on trips north from Ohio into Wisconsin or Michigan and getting excited upon seeing the first white trunks of paper birch trees. Even now I get the same feeling when I drive from the mountainous Mogollon rim north of Phoenix into the Sonoran Desert and see the first saguaro cactus. I anticipate something changing. I realize I'm entering a new environment where it may be colder, hotter, wetter, or drier.

Regardless of how exciting it is initially, the change becomes the norm after a while, rather ho-hum. There are thousands of birch trees or saguaros. The excitement of newness and change disappears, and I start taking the surrounding conditions and scenery for granted. One way I've learned to overcome this tendency is to study the surroundings more closely. As I learn to identify the local plants and animals, study their habits, and join with others who have similar interests, my enthusiasm is restored.

Sounds a lot like a faith walk, doesn't it? Newfound faith can burn with the fire of the Holy Spirit, but it takes the disciplines of prayer, Scripture reading, study, fasting, and meeting with other believers to sustain the excitement of living the Christian life. Just as study, field experience, and joining with other naturalists help open my eyes and ears to the specialness of each ecosystem, spiritual disciplines keep the fire burning and give me the eyes to see the ongoing work of Jesus in my life and the lives of those around me.

Week 4 /Day 5

STIRRED UP

Therefore I remind you to stir up the gift of God, which is in you through the laying on of my hands. For God has not given us a spirit of fear, but of power and of love and of a sound mind. 2 Timothy 1:6-7 NKJV

The shallow little lake near my house in Michigan is host to several cormorants. These big diving birds have large wingspans and are heavier than the average water bird. When these dark-winged divers hit the lake, they go hard and deep, stirring up the muddy bottom in their search for fish. This creates black trails in the water that remain for some time, making it easy to see where the cormorants have been.

Christians are called to stir up the Spirit through prayer, praise, and interacting with other believers. The gathering on Pentecost of the apostles and other believers in prayer opened the way for arrival of the Holy Spirit and the birth of the church (Acts 2:1-4; 4:31). Without the stirring of the ingredients of faith, the Holy Spirit will remain dormant in our lives, and we will fail to make a mark for Christ in the world.

Yet if we dive deep, we will leave trails of God's love, mercy, and forgiveness behind us as we travel on our way to heaven.

This Coming Week

Try centering prayer for 5 minutes each day. This is a meditative way of praying by focusing on a word or phrase from Scripture and waiting in quietness of mind and body for God to come along side you. More specific information on centering prayer is available online.

SEPTEMBER DEVOTIONS

Contents:

Week 1 /Day 1

TEARS OF CREATION

We know that the whole creation has been groaning in labor pains until now. Romans. 8:22 NRSV

Scientists have been pointing out for decades that we are abusing our God-given Earth through excessive use of fossil fuels with the resultant warming of the atmosphere. The Earth's climate is now warmer than it's been for over 800,000 years. One serious consequence of this global warming is the melting of glaciers and ice packs worldwide. Summer arctic ice will soon be a thing of the past. Antarctic ice is melting at a phenomenal rate, as are glaciers in all major mountain ranges from the Andes to the Himalayas.

Melting glaciers are raising sea levels and are already causing increased flooding problems in many coastal areas. Also, many human populations dependent upon glacier melt waters are at risk of water shortages if those glaciers disappear. The Earth is tortured, and tears are flowing, yet we seem only vaguely aware or concerned.

Creation care advocates have been preaching for years that God has charged us with taking care of the garden (Genesis 15:1). I confess that I along with most Christians have done little to live more lightly on God's Earth over these past three or four decades. The time is rapidly approaching when it will be too late to repent (change direction) because various feedback loops in the climate will take over, negating our efforts to stop a spiral towards catastrophe. We need to examine our lives and how we use God's earthly provisions. It is time to love our children, our children's children, and all our future neighbors by turning as much as possible away from our selfish and wasteful lifestyles.

Week 1 /Day 2

CREATION'S MUSIC

All the Earth bows down to you; they sing praise to you, they sing praise to your name. Psalm. 66:4

The soothing sound of flowing water rippling over rocks often is used to facilitate meditation or even to lull people to sleep. An acquaintance of mine once recounted a wonderful act of meditation he had near a small brook. As he listened to the sound of the water flowing over and around the rocks, he could discern many different tones. The sounds blended into a natural music, making his meditation that much easier.

Humans can praise the Lord by speaking, singing, and playing music. Yet even the Lord's inanimate creations can praise Him. Consider the fact that trees clap their hands (Isaiah 55:12), the heavens have voice (Psalm 19), and God can even make the stones shout His praises (Luke 19:40).

What a miracle that we can be here on God's earth and perceive this testimony of creation! Water is a miracle with its life-sustaining substance, rocks are miracles, the air carrying sound waves is a miracle, and the human body's ability to hear is a miracle.

Take time to listen to and savor the sounds of creation. Bubbling brooks, singing birds, buzzing insects, rolling thunder . . . all this and more are audible praises being lifted to the Creator!

Week 1 /Day 3

MORNING FOG

While Aaron was speaking to the whole Israelite community, they looked toward the desert, and there was the glory of the Lord appearing in a cloud. Exodus 16:10

I remember early one September morning walking by an open field near our house. A fog bank drifted slowly over the field in the quiet early morning air. As the fog moved, it changed shape and rose higher, partially obscuring a tree-covered wooded hillside on the opposite side of the field. With sunrise, the fog continued to drift upward and slowly dissipate. The mysterious beauty of the fog-shrouded landscape soon disappeared, but I felt blessed to have witnessed its presence in the early morning quiet.

The Bible often relates how the power and mystery of God is associated with or shrouded in a cloud. Moses heard from God in a cloud on Mount Sinai (Exodus 19:9), God guided the Israelites through the desert with a cloud by day (Exodus 40:38), God spoke from a cloud at the Transfiguration (Matthew 17:5), and Jesus will return upon the clouds (Matthew 24:30).

I'm not a morning person, but I'm convinced that a morning devotional time is important in our faith walk with the Lord. Often things are revealed in the quiet of earlier hours before the hubbub and noise of the world drown out our ability to experience the holy. If you haven't yet set aside some morning devotion time to be with the Lord, maybe now is the time to do it. Sometimes the "Glory of the Lord" passes by in the holiness of the early morning quiet. Don't miss it!

Week 1 /Day 4

CHRISTIAN CONDENSATION

Where there are two or three gathered in my name, there am I in the midst of them. Matthew 18:20 KJV

Watching the development of thunderheads on a hot summer afternoon is fascinating. Small cumulus clouds slowly start to build up in size as atmospheric moisture rises, and warm air condenses on microscopic particles of dust. Once the process starts, it seems to speed up, with the cloud becoming larger at the base and growing higher into the atmosphere. Soon the bottom of the cloud becomes grayer and darker as the tiny droplets of moisture condense and form larger drops.

Before long, streaks of rain can be seen coming from the bottom of the cloud. Distant rolling thunder can be heard as the cloud continues to build, eventually forming mares' tails of high thin clouds in the upper atmosphere that become the characteristic anvil of the thunderhead. As cold air rushes out from the cloud's base— hang on for the coming downpour!

Frank Laubach, a famous missionary who promoted literacy and encouraged living a life of continual prayer, said, "Units of prayer combined, like drops of water, make an ocean which defies resistance." When Christians purposefully unite in prayer, those prayers condense like water droplets forming a thunderstorm, and God's voice becomes audible to a spiritually hearing-impaired world (Psalm 29).

Yes, it's important to have a strong personal prayer life, but it is also important to participate in a strong communal prayer life. Christians united in prayer become God's agents of change in the world. When God shows up, hang on! As Psalm 29 describes, His voice breaks the cedars, shakes the desert, twists the oaks, strips the leaves from the trees, and floods the place. But in the end, He brings strength and peace to His people.

Week 1 / Day 5

CLIMATE CHANGE AND PROPHECY

The Earth is defiled by its people; they have disobeyed the laws, violated the statutes and broken the everlasting covenant. Isaiah 24:5

During one of my early morning walks in the neighborhood, I witnessed a particularly memorable sunrise. Just before the sun appeared above the horizon, high cirrus clouds reflected a pinkish light over the landscape and the earth seemed to glow in the diffuse light.

Scientists say that climate change is causing the lower atmosphere to warm while the upper atmosphere is cooling, which could result in more high cloud formations. This made me think of the Old Testament prophets and the gift of prophecy. Just as the clouds were able to cast light prior to the sun rising, the prophets' words often cast light on the future. Biblical prophecy is both foretelling (predictive) and forthtelling (preaching or teaching how to live in the here and now).

Suspected causes of climate change are related to many of the same cultural issues addressed by the Old Testament prophets—false cultural idols (in our case unbridled consumerism), social injustices (the poorest of the world are most adversely affected by climate change) and fouling of God's good earth through selfishness. As so often documented in the Old Testament, we can choose to ignore the warnings of the prophets, but we do so at our—and future generations'—peril.

This Coming Week

Think about your role in climate change. Almost everything we do has some impact—driving, flying, the types of foods we eat, the size of our houses, what we do for recreation, etc.

Week 2 /Day 1

DOUG

Also, seek the peace and prosperity of the city to which I have carried you into exile. Pray to the Lord for it, because if it prospers, you too will prosper. Jeremiah 29:7

My wife and I recently bought a condominium bordering a little lake separated from a small creek by a man-made dike. The condo development is located on a tract of land in western Michigan that was once a celery farm. In fact, the lake itself was a former celery field that the condo developer flooded.

A few months after moving into our condo, we noticed what looked like a campfire in a wooded area across the lake. One day, my wife and I stopped by the area on a walk and met Doug sitting by a small fire pit. Doug's family had owned the celery farm and had sold it to the condo developer on a land contract. Unfortunately, a severe economic downturn resulted in the developer going bankrupt and left Doug's family without the income they had counted on—money that was to be used for their retirement years.

Besides a modest home in town, Doug retained ownership of the tiny wedge of land between the far end of the lake and the creek where he created his campsite. There, despite his economic disappointments, he could spend a day close to the land he once owned and farmed.

The Israelites were heartbroken when they were taken into Babylonian captivity. (Psalm 137:2, "There on the poplars we hung our harps.") However, God's word to the Israelites was to make themselves at home in Babylon (Jeremiah 29:4-9), which they did, despite their unfamiliarity with the place. God can be worshipped in spirit anywhere, as Jesus made clear to those who thought that worship could only occur in familiar places (the Temple). A new covenant would take the place of the old.

Although we may be uncomfortable with changes in place of residence, careers, health, family, etc., God goes with us wherever we end up, even before we arrive. He invites us to make ourselves at home wherever we are by putting our trust in Him.

Week 2 /Day 2

MAKING CONTACT

"Do not come any closer," God said. "Take off your sandals, for the place where you are standing is holy ground." Exodus 3:5

When God spoke from the burning bush, He instructed Moses to take off his sandals because he was standing on holy ground (Exodus 3:5). By taking off his sandals, Moses became more vulnerable to the hot desert sand, scorpions, and thorns, but by standing barefoot—trusting in the Lord—his excuses for not doing God's will melted away. Shoes and boots disguise the vulnerability of our intimacy with creation.

Our separation from God's creation goes far beyond protective footwear. In this post-modern age, we have been phenomenally successful protecting ourselves from the rest of nature. We build mighty cities, transport goods and food long distances using fossil fuels, level ancient forests and mountain tops, and engage in many other activities detrimental to creation's healthy functioning. We spend much more time in front of our TVs and computers than we spend outdoors in touch with nature (with shoes on or off). We've largely lost contact with creation—God's general revelation. We have separated ourselves to the point of losing our appreciation for the importance of God's sustaining provision.

Just as we risk losing contact with the Lord by not praying and reading Scripture regularly, we risk not hearing the Lord concerning the care of His creation by not spending time in it. He has charged us as gardeners (Genesis 2:15), but the scientific indications are that the garden is in trouble. It's time to take off our shoes, stand before the Lord, and drop our excuses for not fulfilling our charge of caring for creation. God is waiting for us to make contact and to follow His directions in caring for what is His (Ps. 24:1). All ground is holy ground.

Week 2 /Day 3

RATTLESNAKE

I will fear no evil, for you are with me; your rod and your staff, they comfort me. Psalm 23:4

Our family group, including our 2-year-old grandson, decided to take an early spring hike in the desert. My wife was in the lead when she suddenly stopped and said she saw something near a creosote bush along the trail. Next, she heard the tell-tail rattle of a diamondback rattlesnake. The whole group stopped, as she slowly backed up. A couple minutes later, the snake slithered across the trail and out of sight.

We were relieved that our little grandson had not been running ahead and seen the snake first, or that the snake had seen him first. Thankfully grandma was leading the way, protecting us.

If we let Jesus lead us down the trails of our lives, we are also protected from spiritual dangers lurking just off the path. Psalm 23 is familiar to many people as something read at funerals, but it really speaks of the Lord's working in our daily lives. He leads us on right paths where we have no fear since He leads with rod and staff. As we trust in Him, we are strengthened, and we can relax and enjoy life even in the presence of trials and tribulations. When we look back along the trail as we arrive at the house of the Lord, we will see mercy and love scattered behind us, marking our way.

Week 2 /Day 4

ASK THE ANIMALS

Because people break all bounds, the land mourns, all who live in it waste away, the beasts of the field and the birds of the air and the fish of the sea are dying. Hosea 4:2-3

In late 2019, the results of a comprehensive assessment of North American bird populations revealed a staggering loss of breeding birds across almost all species. The overall bird population of the continent has decreased by about 3 billion birds since 1970.

The World Wildlife Living Planet Report for 2020 also documented alarming declines in populations of amphibians, mammals, fish, and reptiles. Even many insect and other invertebrate populations have shown serious declines in the past 50 years.

These events are reminiscent of Hosea's prophecy: "Therefore the land will mourn; and everyone who dwells there will waste away with the beasts of the field and the birds of the air; even the fish of the sea will be taken away." (Hosea 4:3)

The animals are telling mankind that something is going very wrong here on God's Earth. Humans are devastating God's good creation. The collective greed and questing for the "good life" are breaking bounds that God has placed on the inhabitants and caretakers of a finite planet. The plundering and polluting of the planet by the wealthy minority is not only harming animal life but also making life even more difficult for the billions of humans having the bare necessities of life.

We need to take a long hard look at the lack of sustainability and the inequities of our society if there is any hope for saving the planet and ourselves. God's provision is sufficient for all people and creatures, but is mankind's love sufficient to the task of living sustainably and justly on this Earth? Jesus makes it clear that God's love extends to everyone and to all creation, and that humankind's love for each other should, as well.

Week 2 /Day 5

OLD BEAN PLANTS

And afterward, I will pour out my Spirit on all people. Your sons and daughters will prophesy, your old men will dream dreams; your young men will see visions. Joel 2:28

Each year I include plenty of bush beans in my spring planting. The beans grow very well in the sandy, rich soil of my garden. Yet after the first heavy crop, the plants quickly decline, and I pull them up.

This year I left the original plants in place and kept them watered. To my amazement the old plants seem to have a second life and, again, produced abundantly despite beetle-chewed and yellowing leaves.

It was a good lesson. At 75 years old, I sometimes feel like an old bean plant, well past the prime of my production—my leaves yellowing around the edges—but maybe not yet ready for the compost heap. God still wants me to be put to use—to produce for Him. I'm blessed with enough health to continue gardening and donating fresh, healthful green beans to local food banks, just one way God will use an old man and a bunch of bean plants.

My prayer is to be drenched in His Spirit and to continue not only dreaming dreams but to help His dreams for others come true.

This Coming Week

Go to the U.S. Fish and Wildlife Service's website and search for a listing of endangered species, remembering that every species plays some role in the web of life that God created here on Earth.

Week 3 /Day 1

SHEET WEAVERS

Unless you see signs and wonders, you will not believe. John 4:48

As I look across the neighborhood lawns on late summer and early fall mornings, I often see dew collected on spider webs spun by a group of spiders known as sheet weavers. The webs are attached to the tops of grass blades and are horizontal to the ground.

The dew-soaked webs remind me of the story in Judges (6:36-40) where Gideon, hesitant to lead Israel against the Midianites, asked God for a sign involving fleece placed on the ground. Gideon's first request was that there would be dew on the fleece and not on the ground. Then he asked for dew on the ground and not on the fleece. It seems like Gideon was asking God for a sign of his worthiness. He was worried about leading under his own power rather than under God's power. God verified His call to Gideon by granting his requests.

Gideon's story reminds me of my own struggles. How do I discern between a real call from the Lord and my own ideas of what I should be doing? This is not an easy question for any of us, and the answer is usually only found through a strong prayer life—not putting fleece out on the lawn! Sometimes the Lord will provide a clear sign to confirm an answer, but more often we must just press on working out our faith walk in "fear and trembling" (Philippians 2:12).

Week 3 /Day 2

EQUINOX

But do not overlook this one fact, beloved, that with the Lord one day is as a thousand years, and a thousand years as one day. 2 Peter 3:8 NRSV

Humans have long observed spring and fall equinoxes in the Northern Hemisphere as evidenced by sites such as Stonehenge in England and Mayan ruins in Mexico at Chichen Itza.

For millennia, the Jewish nation has observed Passover based on the first full moon after the spring equinox. Passover is when the passion and death of Jesus took place. This is why we, as Christians, set the date of Easter based roughly on Jewish Passover dates.

Various calendars and ways of calculating time's passage have been invented and revised throughout history. My wife and I sponsor a child in Ethiopia, where the calendar is always 7 to 8 years behind the Gregorian calendar that we use. And even the Gregorian calendar needs tweaking with a leap year every fourth year.

For all this focusing on dates and feast days, God is beyond time, and we don't really need specific dates and times to worship Him. He has always been available, is always available, and will always be available for us to worship and adore, until the day we too will be with Him beyond all calendars and time.

Week 3 /Day 3

LATE BLOOMERS

In old age they still produce fruit; they are always green and full of sap. Psalm 92:14 NRSV

Here in the Midwest where I live, wild asters and witch-hazel shrubs bloom long after all the spring and summer flowers have peaked and declined with the approach of fall. Despite their lateness in appearance, the cerulean blue of asters and the pale yellow of tiny witch-hazel flowers brighten an increasingly dark season.

In mid-summer the asters would be overlooked—just be another pretty flower—and the tiny witch-hazel blossoms would probably not be noticed. Just as peaks of blue sky and rays of sunlight are welcomed amid dreary late fall afternoons, so too are these late-blooming flowers.

At over 75 years old, I have been blessed with good health, for which I'm thankful. I am also feeling at my age the need to better reflect the Lord's grace to others around me. I don't mean in brilliant splashes of color and fragrance; I just need to find more ways to bring a little more of the Lord's overlooked brightness—asters and witch-hazel— into the world.

Week 3 /Day 4

BREATH

And with that He breathed on them and said, "Receive the Holy Spirit." John 20:22

I was struggling with lots of indecision in my life, trying to figure things out on my own. Although I had been praying for discernment and wisdom every morning, I didn't seem to hear anything from God.

Then, as I took my usual solitary early morning walk along a nearby field, I noticed a speck of yellow in the dewy grass. Looking more closely, I saw it was a small sulfur butterfly immobilized by the cool morning temperature.

I carefully picked up the tiny creature and held it gently in my hand. As I blew warm breath on it, the butterfly slowly began to move and flutter its wings. After several minutes, I opened my hand and this one little piece of God's beautiful creation flew off into the morning.

The transition of the butterfly from being immobilized by the cold to flying off after experiencing the warmth of my hand and breath made me think how the hand of God and the breath of the Holy Spirit could free me from being frozen in indecision. Instead of trying to move ahead on my own power and trying to use strictly my own logic, I needed the power of the Holy Spirit. I began praying more to hear the Spirit rather than telling God what I wanted and asking him to make it happen.

Turning my life decisions over to the Lord frees me from the paralysis of indecision rooted in fear. As Isaiah 26:3 states, "Thou shall keep him in perfect peace, whose mind is stayed on thee, because he trusteth in thee."

Week 3 /Day 5

THE TRINITY TREE

Therefore go and make disciples of all nations, baptizing them in the name of the Father and of the Son and of the Holy Spirit, and teaching them to obey everything I have commanded you. Matthew 28:19

In discussing biological complexity, ecologist Frank Egler once said that "ecosystems are not only more complex than we think, they are more complex than we can think." Trinitarianism, or the belief in three persons in one God, is a tenant of Christian faith and is truly a concept more complex than we can think.

Ever since Jesus commissioned the disciples to baptize in the name of the Father, and of the Son, and of the Holy Spirit (Matthew 28:19), theologians and other Christians have struggled to understand the concept of "three in one." It seems counterintuitive. Faith provides us with a way to believe in a God bigger than what we can humanly understand. In fact, God is bigger than the known and unknown universe.

Instead of trying to reason a way to an understanding of Trinity, just look to the sassafras tree—a common woodland tree of eastern North America. It's one of the only trees that bear three distinctly shaped leaves—simple oval leaves, mitten-shaped leaves, and three-lobed leaves—all on one tree. Each leaf is part of the tree and functions both on its own and in connection with the tree as a whole. No one shape of leaf is more important than the others in its biological role of photosynthesis.

A sassafras tree with only one kind of leaf would not be the same. Perhaps if sassafras had been native to Israel, Jesus might have used it to explain the Trinity!

This Coming Week

Meditate on this thought, "A thousand years in your sight are like a day that has just gone by, or like a watch in the night." Psalm 90:4

Week 4 /Day 1

HARVESTING WHAT WE DIDN'T PLANT

If someone strikes you on one cheek, turn to him the other also. If someone takes your cloak, do not stop him from taking your tunic. Give to everyone who asks of you, and if anyone takes what belongs to you, do not demand it back. Luke 6:29-30

My sugar baby watermelons were just about ready to pick, but I was going on vacation for a few days so I thought I'd let them stay on the vine until I got back. When I returned a few days later, I excitedly rushed to the garden to retrieve the fruit. Imagine my dismay when I discovered the melons were gone!

Someone had helped themselves to my melons, which, unfortunately, often happens in community gardens. My first thought was that some lazy so-and-so was enjoying the fruits of my hard work. I had been taken advantage of once again. Viewed from the perspective of human justice, there was a crime committed and commission of a crime calls for punishment of the guilty.

Once I calmed down a little, I tried to keep in mind that Jesus was not a big proponent of the human justice system. He tells us to "turn the other cheek" in Matthew 5:39 and advises, "If someone takes your coat, give him your shirt as well" (Luke 6:27). Giving (and even being taken advantage of) is part of Jesus's way of showing unconditional love. As stated in Isaiah 55:8-9, God's thoughts are not our thoughts.

So who am I to care about a couple of missing watermelons—after all, if the thief was caught and brought to me, what punishment should I seek out for this person? As a follower of Jesus, I might think the very best response would be, why didn't you pick the green beans?

In my humanness, I would prefer a tough love approach in this situation—confronting what I view as a wrong and not becoming a doormat, but is that what Jesus would do? Would that be true agape love? I don't have the answer.

Week 4 /Day 2

THE DEPTHS

The words of a man's mouth are deep waters; the fountain of wisdom is a bubbling brook. Proverbs 18:4

I decided to try fly-fishing a few years after my retirement. I enjoy the challenge of reading water, selecting the right fly pattern, and bringing in and releasing beautiful fish. The object of fishing is to fool the fish. Just as, often in our culture, the basis for human interaction is not being totally honest with each other.

In the first half of Proverbs 18:4, the writer reflects on how our talk may or may not match our thoughts. We often can't fathom the "deep waters" of one's words knowing for sure another's motives. Proverbs warns us not to be naïve and believe every word we hear. We are, sadly, a conniving species, as was shown so clearly in the Garden of Eden. We delude ourselves as well as those around us. This is the opposite of God's Word, which is a fountain of wisdom and says what it means.

As the beginning words of the 1940s radio show, "The Shadow" stated, "Who knows what evil lurks in the hearts of men?" The Lord knows and it's only through wading into His wisdom that we can truly see ourselves and others for what we are—flawed but loved children of God.

Week 4 /Day 3

INHABITED

He did not create it to be empty but founded it to be inhabited.
Isaiah 45:18

As a biologist by training, the diversity and adaptability of life has always amazed me. Plants, animals, bacteria, and other microorganisms inhabit just about every possible niche on Earth, from huge baleen whales swimming the ocean to bacteria and fungi living under Antarctic ice. Even our bodies are the ecological niches for hundreds of species of microorganisms living in and on us. *Demodex* mites, for example, carry on a satisfactory and usually undetected life right in the pores of our noses!

In Genesis, God saw all life as very good and blessed it, making it sacred. Life on Earth is abundant, miraculously diverse, and ever moving through cycles of birth and death.

As Paul states in Colossians 1:17 and is reiterated by John in Revelation 4:11, all life (and the non-living world) was created through and is held together in Christ. The creation, including all life, reflects the Creator and deserves our respect. As the Christian environmental scientist Cal DeWitt has said, "the extinction of a living species is equivalent to ripping a page out of Scripture." Our job as stewards of creation is to tend the garden (Genesis 2:15) and treat all life respectfully as a creation of God.

Week 4 /Day 4

MIMICRY

Be perfect, therefore, as your heavenly Father is perfect. Matthew 5:48

This past September, I was watching monarch butterflies heading south as they do every fall all over the United States and Canada. Long-distance migration makes them susceptible to predation from birds. However, birds soon learn not to eat the brightly colored orange and black Monarchs since the butterflies contain an apparently bad-tasting toxin. The toxin originates from milkweed plants that are the exclusive host plants of Monarch caterpillars.

Viceroy butterflies mimic the appearance of the Monarchs. Birds that have had a bad gastronomic encounter with a Monarch will also keep a distance from Viceroys even though Viceroys are not toxic. In the case of Viceroys, they "look the part" of a Monarch and use it to their advantage. Mimicry is a type of trickery found many places in nature. In a sense, it's where one creature has the image but not the likeness of another creature.

Humans are made in the image and likeness of God. Jesus is the perfect image of God as He states in John 14:9, "Anyone who has seen me has seen the Father." Jesus is also the perfect likeness of God being perfect in love. He is the real thing. My prayer is to be more and more both the image AND the likeness of God.

Week 4 /Day 5

FOREVER WATER

"But those who drink of the water that I will give them will never be thirsty. The water that I will give will become in them a spring of water gushing up to eternal life" John 4:14 NRSV

The total amount of water on Earth has remained the same for billions of years. Scientists still are uncertain about the origin of all this water. One theory is that water-containing comets and asteroids bombarded the Earth. Another theory is that much of the water was formed within the Earth through various physical and chemical processes. This reminds me of the Genesis account of water "welling up from the depths" as well as "raining down from above."

Regardless of origin, water is an absolute necessity for life, as we know it. Water constantly moves through the atmosphere, in the form of oceans, lakes, glaciers, icecaps, air (clouds), organic bodies, and us. Our thirst for water is never totally quenched since our bodies are constantly losing water. The molecules in our glass of water have passed through many different forms and served many different purposes over the millennia.

Without an ongoing connection with the water of life available through the Holy Spirit, our souls remain thirsty and unsatisfied, and our faith can shrivel. Like physical water, living spiritual water is available in many different forms that can help us stay hydrated no matter where we are on our journey back to the original source.

This Coming Week

Be mindful of how precious and ancient the water is in your drinking glass. Look up Christian charities like Lifewater International whose mission is to provide clean water to the underserved in the developing world.

OCTOBER DEVOTIONS

Contents:

Week 1 /Day 1

PRAIRIE FIRE

Let both of them grow together until the harvest; and at harvest time I will tell the reapers, Collect the weeds first and bind them in bundles to be burned, but gather the wheat into my barn. Matthew 13:30 NRSV

Although most of the native short-grass and long-grass prairies of the American Midwest and Great Plains have disappeared under the plow and development, remnants of these biomes still exist in scattered, protected areas. These native prairie plants have deep root systems and have adapted to periodic fires that consume surface vegetation.

A prairie fire purges non-native and shallow-rooted invasive plants while opening the soil surface to more sunlight. Fire also fertilizes the soil with ash from burned plant material. The deep roots of prairie plants remain untouched by fire and soon sprout new growth.

As Christians, we strive to plant our roots of faith deep into the love of Christ. In this way, the Lord enables us to survive and even thrive through the fires of life and to "sprout" into the 'Sonshine' of eternal life.

Week 1 /Day 2

MORNING REFLECTIONS ON THE SUN

Be still, and know that I am God. Psalm 46:10

Early morning walks often provide opportunities to experience the power of the sun in more subtle ways than can be experienced during bright afternoons. One fall Saturday after an October frost, I strolled out in the yard, passing under some sugar maples still holding most of their red and yellow leaves. The wind was still, and the morning sun was bright in the blue October sky. As I walked under the trees, I heard (and felt) drops of water dripping from the leaves as the sun melted their covering of frost.

Another morning I observed a small buckeye tree in a nearby park that seemed to have a smoking trunk. In this case, the rays of the morning sun were vaporizing moisture from the dark-colored bark.

One late winter morning before the Sun rose, I noticed that the light snow of the night before remained on the street only in places that had been shaded by trees or buildings the day before. The rest of the pavement retained enough warmth from the previous day to melt the snow.

When we are born again of the Spirit, we experience something close to the full power of Jesus's sun. A manifestation of this kind of experience is what happened to the apostles on the first Pentecost as described in Acts 2. However, it's in our daily walk with the Lord that we must become attuned to the constant, but often subtle, working and power of the Holy Spirit. Just as the early morning mellowness of the sun impacts the natural world in small ways around us, so too does the Spirit often work quietly in the transforming of our lives.

Week 1 /Day 3

LEAF PILES

Every day they continued to meet in the temple courts. They broke bread in their homes and ate together with glad and sincere hearts, praising God and enjoying the favor of all people. Acts 2:46

I love autumn mornings when I can stroll out the door and smell freshly fallen leaves while hearing the call of blue jays. However, I've never been particularly fond of one fall chore: raking leaves.

Many times, while laboring away in my yard, I'll just manage to get a number of leaf piles raked together ready to pick up when a late morning breeze will kick up, bringing down more leaves and scattering loose leaves on the ground. Although this can be very frustrating, I've observed that leaves already in piles resist being blown since their irregular edges often interlock with each other, keeping them together.

The wind resistance of leaves piled together reminds me of a sermon I once heard about how there are no "lone ranger" Christians. Being a Christian means being in community, holding each other together in love and accountability, thereby resisting the forces of the world that would have you believe you can make it on your own.

Although most of us do not live in the type of Christian community described in Acts 2: 42-47, we still need to interact frequently with others in our faith community. Alone we can easily be blown away by the temptations, worries, and fears of the world, but joined together in faith we can remain strong. Like the autumn leaves, we can continue to bear the fruits of the Spirit despite any "winds" that gust through our lives.

Week 1 /Day 4

HOLD BACK

The King will reply, "I tell you the truth, whatever you did for the one of the least of these brothers of mine, you did for me." Matthew 25:40

There is no doubt that we in the United States are a consumer society. In fact, we are the biggest consumers on Earth. We are surrounded by a swirl of multi-media commercialism telling us how much better our lives would be if we only bought some particular product. Economists and government officials continually tell us what we need to do to be good consumers including increasing our consumption to keep the economy going. As a result of globalization, many countries worldwide are, unfortunately, following this same pattern. Our capitalistic lust for more stuff leads to less of life's bare essentials for many of our poorer brothers and sisters throughout the world.

As Christians, we need to stand against a level of consumption that damages God's Earth and deprives many of His children of life's necessities. I'm reminded of an approach that my wife's family used when they had company for dinner and some of the serving dishes were running low. They would whisper to each other "FHB" (for "family hold back"), thus making sure that guests had enough.

As part of the worldwide Christian family, we need to show restraint in our personal consumption. In this way, we can redirect the time and money saved toward helping others less fortunate who are also guests at God's table. In this interconnected world, we need to understand how our lifestyles impact others and to recall Jesus' admonition of caring for the least of these (Matthew 25:37-40). Let's learn to pass the plate of God's blessings on to all of God's children in an atmosphere of FHB.

Week 1 /Day 5

IN SEASON AND OUT OF SEASON

Preach the Word; be prepared in season and out of season; correct, rebuke and encourage—with great patience and careful instruction. 2 Timothy 4:2

Spotted knapweed was accidentally introduced in imported grass seed from Europe in the early 1900s. This plant can now be found in much of the United States. It grows in great profusion in the fields near my Michigan home. The pretty blue blossoms are pleasing to the eye, but it's a noxious weed that's very aggressive in its growth. It can quickly take over large areas of land, crowding out native species.

Most knapweed plants bloom in midsummer and then die back, but as long as the weather stays warm and there is enough moisture, a few plants will continue blooming right up to a killing frost or freeze. Such blossoming and seed production on the part of a small number of plants after the main growing season is characteristic of several other weeds, such as Canada goldenrod, dandelions, and Queen Ann's lace.

Paul instructed Timothy to be prepared "in season and out of season" to preach the Gospel. None of us know when the "killing frost" might come and end our earthly existence, and really, it should make no difference. Like the weeds, we need to keep on blooming, and spreading seeds of faith, hope, and love whether it's early, mid, or late season. Whether you're a plant or a Christian, "keep on keeping on" is the key to victorious living!

This Coming Week

Consider a partial fast over one day during the week. Prayerfully consider the issue of hunger in the world and even in your own town. What might you be able to do about it?

Week 2 /Day 1

THE BODY OF CHRIST

Speaking the truth in love, we will in all things grow up into Him who is the Head, that is, Christ. From Him the whole body, joined and held together by every supporting ligament, grows and builds itself up in love, as each part does its work. Ephesians 4:15-16

Aspens are the beautiful light-barked trees often photographed in mountainous and northern areas of North America. Their whitish bark often contrasts with surrounding dark evergreen trees. In the fall, their leaves turn golden yellow, setting them apart from the other trees.

Large stands of aspen are usually the result of one initially established tree and are all genetically identical. Aspens send out lateral roots that then form sprouts and eventually develop into another tree. The aspen stand expands as this process continues. However, the rooting and sprouting can only occur when the already established trees are healthy and producing plenty of carbohydrates for growth.

Church growth has some similarities to the growth of aspen groves. The Church is founded by One (Christ), and it has been sending out "lateral roots" through evangelism since the first Pentecost, as described in Acts 2. All believers have the same genetic Spirit—"we are one in the Spirit" (Ephesians 4:4). Church growth only occurs through prayer, worship, and service and when believers nurture each other and new "sprouting" members and congregations (Ephesians 4:16 and James 3:18).

As with a healthy grove of aspens amid a pine-covered mountainside, the beauty of a healthy Church can stand out in contrast to the darkness of the surrounding world.

Week 2 /Day 2

BLUE SKY

I saw the Lord, high and exalted, seated on a throne; and the train of his robe filled the temple. Isaiah 6:1

As I think of this passage, I visualize the train of God's robe as big and blue as the sky. In biblical times, blue-dyed cloth was very rare and expensive, and its use was largely restricted to priestly garments. Sea snails were the source of the blue dye. However, it took a huge number of snails and a very smelly process to produce relatively little dye.

Several years ago, my seven-year-old grandson and I were talking about why the sky is blue. I mistakenly thought that the blue color was caused by sunlight passing through dust and moisture in the air. The color actually results from the way atmospheric nitrogen and oxygen absorb and diffuse more blue and violet light than they do colors toward the red end of the light spectrum.

A color once so difficult for people to make is an extravagantly used color in creation. God cloaks His temple (the Earth) in a robe of extravagantly deep blue sky every day that His Sun shines through life-giving air. God is not only the Creator of the air we breathe, but also an extravagant painter with many palettes to create beauty throughout His creation.

Week 2 /Day 3

ABSCISSION LAYERS

Jesus answered, "If you want to be perfect, go, sell your possessions and give to the poor, and you will have treasure in heaven. Then come, follow me." Matthew 19:21 ERV

As late summer and early fall days become shorter, leaf stems on deciduous trees form abscission layers. These corky thick cells eventually cut off the nutrient supply to the leaves, thereby causing leaves to change color and eventually fall from the tree. This annual leaf drop is vital for tree survival during the winter, and it is only through the formation of abscission layers that these trees can shed their strongly attached leaves.

We humans can get awfully attached to things—habits, possessions, titles, money, or power, to name a few. Jesus calls us to loosely hold all the things of this world so that they do not replace the treasures of heaven. He knew that our hearts follow what we treasure and that clinging to the things of this world brings bondage (Matthew 6:21).

Few of us are called to vows of poverty or a monastic lifestyle, but our Christian faith calls all of us to develop abscission layers that will enable us to give up whatever is necessary in our lives to follow Jesus. We are called to cling to the Good News above all else in life. Only when we stand ready to let anything go for the cause of Christ can we be truly free (John 8:32). What are you holding on to?

October

Week 2 /Day 4

BEAUTY IN DEATH

Now we know that if the earthly tent we live in is destroyed, we have a building from God, an eternal house in heaven. 2 Corinthians 5:1

A mosaic of freshly fallen multicolored leaves covered the trail. Although the leaves were dead, they still held beauty. The vivid shades of red, yellow, orange, and gold appeared lively, but I knew they would soon turn brown and decay into the earth.

As we grow old, we say that we are in "the autumn of life," and eventually, the ravages of age and disease will result in physical death. While it may not be pretty, an understanding of physical death in terms of nature's cycles reveals a beauty in God's design. While our physical lives are subject to these natural cycles, our spiritual lives are not.

Until we accept Christ as our Savior, we are stalled in the dead of winter as far as our spiritual lives are concerned. But by placing our trust in Jesus and the one "beautiful" death He suffered for us, we also will encounter death as beautiful and receive eternal life in Him. When the earthly tent of our bodies fails through physical death, we will move into the temple of God. That's beautiful.

Week 2 /Day 5

SILENCE

When he opened the seventh seal, there was silence in heaven for about a half hour. Revelation 8:1

A late summer rain had stopped, and fluffy white-gray cumulus clouds slowly drifted across an azure sky. My wife and I had just portaged our canoe into one of the remote lakes of the Boundary Waters area of northern Minnesota. As our canoe glided across the glassy surface of the lake in a calm wind, we lifted our paddles and listened. It was absolutely quiet—no bird song, no wind in the trees, no distant noise from human activity. The only sound was an occasional drop of water falling into the lake off our lifted paddles. We didn't speak for a long while as we just soaked in this sacred moment.

Sometimes words cannot convey nor can music or any other human sound express our awe of the majesty and power of God. Our ability to create sound fails us as we stand in silence in front of the Lord of the Universe. "The Lord is in His holy temple; let all Earth be silent before Him." Habakkuk 2:20

While it may seem difficult in our everyday noisy world, it is good to seek a time of silence before God each day, to acknowledge what is sacred. To be still is to know that God in His wholeness (holiness), to know God as God (Psalm 46:10). Find some time to experience the beauty of silence before God.

This Coming Week

Look at some of your favorite things—an item of clothing, an expensive fishing rod, a new kitchen appliance, etc. How difficult would it be to give that item away?

October

Week3 /Day 1

EARTH SONG

Sing to the Lord, all the earth; proclaim his salvation day after day.
1 Chronicles 16:23

A cacophony of sound constantly emanates from Earth—billions of birds singing, trillions of insects buzzing and singing, millions of frogs and toads croaking, rolling thunder from thousands of thunderstorms, crashing waterfalls, babbling brooks, rolling surf, rumbling volcanoes—not to mention a myriad of sounds of human speech and activity. We live in the ultimate Surround Sound, with God's beautiful, life-filled blue marble spinning through silent space singing to itself.

As aptly stated in Max Heindel's quote, "Music is the soul of language," when words alone won't do, music may help. The Bible is full of singing. After escaping from the Egyptians, Miriam wrote the first song recorded in the Bible (Exodus 15:1-21). Many of the Psalms were written as songs associated with temple worship. Song of Songs is a beautiful love song. The Magnificat was Mary's song upon hearing of news of her pregnancy (Luke 1:46-55), and the singing continues around God's throne (Revelation 5:9-10).

Think about all the joyful sounds of creation rising at this very moment from around the earth. It will be hard not to start humming a tune to join the mountains and forests (Isaiah 44:22-23), the sea and the rivers (Psalm 98:7-9) and all creatures (Psalm 148) in their praise of the Creator.

Week 3 /Day 2

BIRD WITH A MESSAGE

As Jesus was coming up out of the water, he saw heaven being torn open and the Spirit descending on Him like a dove. Mark 1:10 NRSV

Last fall, my wife and I were invited by some friends to attend an outdoor camping program called *Opening the Book of Nature.* The purpose of the weekend was to join in prayer, meditation, and sharing with others in the outdoors. My wife was having a lot of doubts about the promises of God in her life. As any Christian knows, doubt can eat away at faith. We thought this retreat would help both of us discover what Nature's Author might have to say about things.

We traveled to a site in southeastern Ohio on a beautiful fall day in October. After getting settled in, the group engaged in a short discussion and some Scripture reading around the campfire. After that, all the participants fanned out into the surrounding woods to spend some time alone. My wife found a large log and laid back on it to look up through the colored mosaic of leaves. As she gazed into the blue autumn sky, she felt a deep peace come over her. Then a shadow startled her as it passed across the leafy canopy above. A large whitish bird circled above her, gliding on the autumn afternoon thermals. She felt she had experienced a sign from God (theophany) confirming His presence and providing her comfort.

Theophanies—manifestations of God in nature—are countless if we learn to see with eyes of faith. God's presence throughout the Bible was often marked by theophanies. The column of cloud guiding the Israelites in the desert (Exodus 13:21), Ezekiel's windstorm (Ezekiel 1:4), the dove at Jesus' baptism (Mark 1:10), and thunder when Jesus predicted His death (John 12:28-29) are just a few examples.

These physical manifestations of God's presence were recorded as lessons for the larger Christian community. But if we have a personal need for a physical manifestation of His presence in our lives and faithfully seek Him, there is no reason to believe He will not provide it. Whether it's a beautiful bird, a sunset, or a kind word or act from a friend or a stranger, God will use whatever is needed.

Week 3 /Day 3

STAYING IN THE WORD

The Lord watches over you—the Lord is your shade at your right hand; the sun will not harm you by day, nor the moon by night.
Psalm 121:5-6

Several years ago, my wife and I decided to read through the Bible in one year. We had a small poodle at the time that loved to catch balls we threw to her. As one of us would sit on the couch and read the Bible aloud, the other would sit on the floor and throw balls to the dog. It was a nice, calming time for the three of us, a good end to the day.

That is, until the evening my wife looked down on my baldhead and told me there was a spot on my scalp. She thought I should have it examined by a doctor. I shrugged off her suggestion at the time, but a month or so later I developed a rash on my arm that demanded attention, so I went to a dermatologist. While talking to the doctor, I mentioned the spot on my head. A biopsy followed, revealing I had early-stage melanoma. Thankfully, it was successfully removed with surgery.

I thank God many times for bringing His Word and our daily routine together, which ultimately saved my life. He even gave me a rash to finally get me to the dermatologist since I was too stubborn to listen to my wife! Ever since that time, I think about how precious it is to "stay in the Word."

Week 3 /Day 4

A LONE PINE

They will have no fear of bad news; their hearts are steadfast, trusting in the LORD. Psalm 112:7

My wife and I usually start our day with a short Bible verse followed by a 5-minute silent meditation time. The room we use for this has windows looking out into a wooded area of mixed pine and deciduous trees.

During the winter I started noticing a single, somewhat scraggly, white pine poking up behind some oaks and maples. The pine was quite visible through the bare branches of these larger trees in front of it. The pine became an object I could focus on during meditation as it stood in the rain, snow, wind, and winter sunshine.

As spring approached, the oaks and maples started to leaf out and by summer, the pine was almost totally hidden from view. Although I knew it stood there in the summer sun and through the summer thunderstorms, I couldn't really focus on it. When fall arrived, the pine re-emerged into view.

When I thought about this tree, the term "steadfastness" came to mind. It continued holding its place in the woods through all seasons, remaining little changed in appearance, even as trees around it changed.

I have a long way to go in being as steadfast in my faith as that pine tree is steadfast in the woods. It's easy to get blinded by the changing world around us and to wander off the path of our faith journey. I often am consumed and depressed by the bad news of the day instead of placing my trust and gaining peace through faith in the Lord. My prayer is for a more steadfast heart for the Good News of Lord.

ALPENGLOW

When Moses came down from Mount Sinai with the two tablets of the Testimony in his hands, he was not aware that his face was radiant because he had spoken with the Lord. Exodus 34:29

Travelers to mountainous regions occasionally witness a phenomenon known as alpenglow. It can only be seen in the moments right before sunrise or immediately after sunset. Indirect sunlight is reflected and scattered in the lower atmosphere by clouds, precipitation, ice crystals, or particulates. Scientific explanations aside, seeing the mountains glow in stunning shades of reddish-pink light is something not soon forgotten.

When Moses descended from Mount Sinai with the Ten Commandments his face was so radiant from his encounter with God that he needed to cover it when he spoke to the Israelites. Unlike alpenglow that only lasts minutes, Moses' afterglow apparently persisted for some time. He was changed by his encounters with the power of God not only spiritually but also physically. His new level of spiritual enlightenment affected his physical impact on the rest of the Israelites.

In a similar manner, encounters with the Lord through prayer and meditation will change us both inside and out. The fire of the Holy Spirit can create a glow of love, compassion, and wisdom. This is then manifested in our lives and in our relationships with others and the world at large. If working from a center of Christ's love in our lives, we can't help but glow.

This Coming Week

Give some thought to reading completely through the Bible. It doesn't need to be in one year or even a several years but developing a discipline to read a certain amount each day will strengthen your faith.

Week 4 /Day 1

HOW BIRDS SPREAD THE WORD

He said to them, "Go into all the world and preach the good news to all creation." Mark 16:15

The place we were renting had no real view of the outdoors. Our kitchen window looked out over a small patio and across an open walkway to an adjacent building. A small hedge of shrubs at the edge of the patio was about all the nature we could see. Although the prospects of attracting birds to this semi-enclosed, sterile, urban environment seemed poor, I had seen a few finches and sparrows fly through the area on occasion. So I bought a small bird feeder for thistle seeds and hung it at the end of the patio.

Several days went by before I finally saw a single house finch at the feeder. Then over the next week, more and more house finches and a few goldfinches started to appear. Soon the feeder was loaded with a raucous gathering of finches every morning and evening. Obviously, the first finch had communicated to others where the feeding bonanza was located.

As Christians, we too have found a spiritual bonanza in the saving grace of Jesus. He even admonishes us that we must spiritually eat His body and drink His blood to attain salvation, and He refers to Himself as the "bread of life."

Do others see us as spiritually well-fed and inquire as to where we get the food? Do we want to share in the feast prepared for us by telling others of the wonderful food we've found? Hopefully, the answer to both questions is yes! There's plenty for us all to be filled.

Week 4 /Day 2

CHURCH IN THE PARK

But who is able to build a temple for Him since the heavens, even the highest heavens cannot contain Him? 2 Chronicles 2:6

Several years ago, we lived near a wooded park that had a small creek running through it. I often walked our dog, Mayzi, in the park early in the morning before I left for work. The walks gave Mayzi some much-needed exercise, but more than that, it provided me with a time of quiet and prayer.

During these walks I discovered a small clearing that overlooked a bend in the creek. A honey locust tree, full of sharp thorns, stood near the entrance to the clearing. Willows and cottonwood trees grew alongside the creek bank. Birds sang from trees and water burbled as it splashed over rocks and gravel.

The place echoed the themes of a church. I saw the thorns on the honey locust as a reminder of Christ's suffering on the cross. The flowing water called to mind purification, bird song praised the Lord, and the nearby fluttering cottonwood leaves clapped their hands in adoration. No church building was needed for this early morning praise service! I felt that I stood on holy ground as I, along with all creation, praised the Lord.

Week 4 /Day 3

FRIVOLOUS BEAUTY

For in Him all things were created: things in heaven and on earth, visible and invisible, whether thrones or powers or rulers or authorities; all things were created by Him and for Him. He is before all things, and in Him all things hold together. Colossians 1:16-17

Every time I visit Phoenix, Arizona, I am impressed by the beauty of the artwork incorporated into the concrete walls and overpasses along the major highways around the city. Geometric Southwestern designs and a variety of subtle earth tone colors are incorporated into these functional structures. Palo verde trees, bougainvilleas, and other flowering shrubs watered by drip irrigation systems also line the roadways.

Some might think that these artistic and horticultural enhancements along a highway are a frivolous waste of funds. However, they add beauty to the mundane and make a statement about the community's value of beauty.

It's easy to look around God's creation here on Earth and wonder why there is so much beauty—much of it without function (to our narrow human point of view). Why the billions or trillions of stars that illuminate the night sky? Wouldn't just a few be sufficient? Why the fantastic mix of pigments in fall leaves? Why shouldn't they all just turn brown? How many snow-capped peaks or beautiful sunsets do we need?

Thankfully, the Creator is not concerned about "frivolous" beauty. He is extravagant and generous at every turn. Martin Luther stated that God writes the gospel in trees, flowers, stars, and clouds, as well as in the Bible. By looking deeply at the beauty of creation we can glimpse the beauty of the Creator and better understand how He can make all things beautiful in His time.

Week 4 /Day 4

BURNING FORESTS

To you, Lord, I call, for fire has devoured the pastures in the wilderness and flames have burned up all the trees of the field. Joel 1:9

Wildfires are increasing in number and intensity around the globe as the effects of climate change take stronger hold on seasonal temperature and precipitation patterns. This is another example of how we are breaking the covenant of being caretakers of God's Earth Garden. Isaiah 24:5 states it directly, "The Earth is defiled by its people."

Most of us in the developed world participate in the defiling of the Earth by wasting resources, spewing pollutants into the air and water, and throwing waste away on a planet where there is no "away." By hurting the Earth we also hurt our brothers and sisters who share this beautiful planet that God made for all of us to enjoy.

As Christians, the basis of whatever we do should be love—love of what God created and called good, and love of our neighbors near and far and even in future generations. We live in an economically unjust world that was created largely by ignoring or purposefully misinterpreting God's Word. Although we cannot change this situation in the short term, we can strive with God's help to create a more just world. "On Earth as it is in heaven," means showing more kindness, and humbly recognizing our failings to truly live with the fire of the Holy Spirit guiding our lives.

Week 4 /Day 5

SCAVENGING

"Yes, Lord," she replied, "but even the dogs under the table eat the children's crumbs." Matthew 15:28

After our 14-year-old poodle died, we began to notice that the kitchen floor seemed to get dirty a lot faster. Obviously, Mayzi had been a little scavenger of kitchen crumbs.

In nature, there are numerous creatures that scavenge as a way of life—vultures, most notably—but also many other opportunistic feeders, like crows and gulls, skunks and coyotes, wolves and bears, and uncountable insects. These opportunists take advantage of whatever food might be readily available to them, whether beside the road, at a landfill, or left by hunters or predators.

In human society, scavenging for food is certainly not something anyone wants to do. We all want a seat at the table where the food is fresh and healthful.

In the past, I've had difficulty understanding the interaction between Jesus and the Canaanite woman in Matthew 15. The passage seemed like an argument in which Jesus was reluctant to use His healing power. In the end Jesus did not "throw her crumbs" of His power and love to scavenge but brought full and immediate healing to the woman's daughter. He was totally impressed by her great faith.

Jesus showed His disciples that He had plenty of love and power to reach beyond the immediate Israeli society. By extension, His love extends to everyone in every place, including you and me. We do not have to scavenge for His love; we have a seat at the table if we just ask for it.

This Coming Week

Keep your eyes open for the seemingly frivolous beauty in your everyday world.

NOVEMBER DEVOTIONS

Contents:

Week 1 /Day 1

THE UNKNOWN DAY

Show me, O Lord, my life's end and the number of my days; let me know how fleeting is my life. Psalm 39:4

We love to celebrate birthdays and look forward to them every year, but we usually don't think about the day and date on which we will die. That date just quietly goes past each year of our lives as we busy ourselves with our everyday and often self-centered existence. We don't like thinking about death and returning to dust (Genesis 3:19) although the Bible strongly recommends keeping it in mind daily (Ecclesiastes 7:2).

As Christians, we have the hope of glory in Christ after death, and death should hold no sting. That's easy to say, but as humans we know that there is a physical sting both in our own dying and in those we love after we die. The usefulness of acknowledging our pending death is that it can spur us on now to do the important tasks of Kingdom work. As Jesus said, we need to work "while we have light" (John 12:35). We also need to remember that someday our physical death day on Earth will be celebrated as our new birthday with the Lord in heaven.

Week 1 /Day 2

FALSE APPEARANCES

Now we see but a poor reflection as in a mirror; then we shall see face to face. 1 Corinthians 13:12

I often walk along a wooded creek where I love to observe the plants and animals through the seasons of the year. Although the area looks natural to most people, it is only a poor reflection of original ecological conditions. Huge trees once covered the area, and the spring-fed creek ran clear through the forests. Today, none of the original forest is left. There are many exotic plant species that have overgrown the area, and most of the springs have dried up due to development. The stream now carries polluted runoff from roads and parking lots. Much of the original beauty of the landscape has been destroyed, yet most people looking at it would not know it since they never knew the area ever looked any different.

The idea of accepting what we see as natural is similar to how we fail to see the effects of sin in our lives and in society at large. As Paul states in 1 Corinthians 13:12, we view ourselves, others, and world around us through a glass, darkly. Growing up and living in our consumer-oriented culture leaves us thinking our lifestyles and cultural values are the norm. Unfortunately, much of what we see and accept is not as God intended. The injustices and immoralities that have become a part of our cultural system do not reflect Kingdom values. Yet we don't perceive this because we accept what we see as normal.

There is a need to pray for discernment and to work towards the Kingdom conditions that God originally intended for us.

Week 1 /Day 3

WINTER WHEAT

We are hard pressed on every side, but not crushed; perplexed, but not in despair; persecuted, but not abandoned; struck down, but not destroyed. 2 Corinthians 4:8-9

Growing up in the Midwest, I was always fascinated by the beautiful dark green of winter wheat fields in the fall. On a dreary November day, when most of nature has turned shades of brown, the spring green of a wheat field is almost iridescent. I know that when spring arrives the same green will peek through melting snows, and soon the wheat will begin its rapid growth as warmer weather arrives. Winter wheat seems to say to winter, "Throw anything at me. I have the promise of springtime."

Paul relates in 2 Corinthians 4:7-12 that we have the power of Jesus to persevere through whatever life throws at us. The green of winter wheat carries the promise of life's summer harvest through the harshness of winter. As Christians, we also carry on the promise of new life in Jesus, despite the harshness of our circumstances or the world around us. Our power to persevere is not our own, but the eternal power source—Jesus Christ.

Week 1 /Day 4

WINTER

*Let us acknowledge the L*ORD*; let us press on to acknowledge Him. As surely as the sun rises, He will appear; He will come to us like the winter rains, like the spring rains that water the earth." Hosea 6:3*

As I sat in our Phoenix winter rental watching the rain, I realized the importance of a rainy winter day to desert life. Winter rains are essential for survival of many plants and animals of the Southwest. Unlike monsoon thunderstorms and cloudbursts of summer, winter rains are usually much gentler and soak into the ground better. The cooler winter temperatures also reduce evaporation from the soil surfaces. Desert blooms of spring wildflowers only happen after a season of sufficient winter rains that trigger germination.

Even in colder climates with snow and ice, winter is important to many fruit and nut trees that require a certain length of time in subfreezing conditions. Without a certain amount of exposure to cold temperatures, there would be no apples, cherries, or tulips.

Winter can be a good time for us as Christians to "hibernate" by soaking in God's love and instruction and growing inwardly. We can read and meditate on Scripture, spend time indoors with friends and family, and attend worship services. These wintertime spiritual experiences will help us bring springtime joy to a world that often resembles a spiritual desert.

Week 1 /Day 5

RED PINES

I will plant in the wilderness cedar . . . Isaiah 41:18 KJV

By the late 1880s, much of forested land in Michigan, Wisconsin, and Minnesota had been clear-cut of native white pine. Lumberjacks satisfying the demand for building materials gave little thought to the long-term damage being caused to the Earth. When the forests were destroyed, most of the wildlife habitat was lost. These cutover areas had severe soil erosion problems, which contributed to silting and water quality problems in streams and lakes.

Many Civilian Conservation Corps (CCC) jobs during the Great Depression involved planting red pines in the deforested areas. If not for CCC labor in replanting these stripped areas, even more would have been lost ecologically. I have a friend who currently works as a seasonal biologist for the Forest Service in Michigan. He is often tasked with surveying stands of those same red pine trees that will be thinned. This allows for better growth of the remaining pines, as well as for other native trees and shrubs growing up within the stand.

Today we are more aware of damage done when forests are not protected or managed properly. We're also more aware of our role as citizens, consumers, and God's children in protecting and preserving not only forests, but also all of God's creation. As Paul states in Romans 8:19, "all creation waits in eager expectation for the sons of God to be revealed." We all have responsibilities as caretakers of God's beautiful garden called Earth.

This Coming Week

Look up the activities of the Arbor Day Foundation in your area, and plan to participate if there is an event planned for the spring.

Week 2 /Day 1

FROSTED GRASS

Gray hair is a crown of splendor, it is attained by a righteous life.
Proverbs 16:31

Although the first fall frost is a harbinger of cold weather, it also gives a soft beauty to the grass, when billions of frost crystals reflect light at sunrise. Even as the grass withers and turns brown, it can reflect beauty. Biblical comparisons of humans to grass include the well-known Psalm 103:13-14: "As for man, his days are like grass, he flourishes like a flower of the field; the wind blows over it and it is gone, and its place remembers it no more." Isaiah 40:6-8 repeats this theme where human life is described as "withering grass" that contrasts with the word of the Lord which stands forever. Peter quotes this passage from Isaiah (1 Peter 1:24-25) but states it in the context of the new life we have in Christ and the Word.

Now, in my retirement years, I think of these verses in light of my own life. How even in autumn, the frost gives a beauty to the grass.

God showers His grace on us just as He "gives birth to the frost from heaven" (Job 38:29)—even (and maybe especially) in the autumn of our lives. Often with age comes more wisdom and time to share God's Good News, which in turn reflects His faithfulness in our lives. Although our hair may be frosted in gray, God's grace can still bring sparkle to our lives and to those around us.

Week 2 /Day 2

VINE AND THE BRANCHES

I am the vine; you are the branches. If you remain in me and I in you, you will bear much fruit; apart from me you can do nothing. John 15:5

As a biologist, I sometimes have difficulty with some of Jesus's parables, like the one about the vine and the branches. It's true that branches and leaves die if cut off from the vine, but the scientist in me knows that a vine cannot thrive without branches and leaves. It's in the leaves where photosynthesis takes place, which results in the continuing ability of the vine to grow.

Christians are the branches and leaves that express the vine—God's presence—in the world. God chooses to use believers to get His will done. Our participation in Kingdom work is what makes the Body of Christ grow.

I was on a retreat years ago where the motto was, "Christ is Counting on You." This is an awesome responsibility that Jesus placed on Christians when He expressed His confidence (John 14:12) that His followers will do "even greater things than these." These greater things are not necessarily greater miracles; rather, they are our ability to spread the Good News farther and wider to the ends of the Earth. Our job is to keep branching out and gaining more and more leaves to do the work of the Father.

Week 2 /Day 3

LESSONS FROM A STREET TREE

By contrast, the fruit of the Spirit is love, joy, peace, patience, kindness, generosity, faithfulness, gentleness, and self-control. Galatians. 5:22 NRSV

I have been involved for many years in a program called Opening the Book of Nature. The goal of the program is to help Christians discover lessons from God's creation through meditative prayer and the leading of the Holy Spirit. Usually, Opening the Book of Nature events take place in more naturally remote settings such as mountain forests, along the seashore, or in the desert.

Although much can be learned praying and meditating in these more remote locations, much can also be learned close to home. Even a small tree along a busy urban sidewalk holds lessons for us. Some of these might may include steadfastness (growing in an environment of poor soil and air pollution), humility (surrounded by towering buildings and the busyness of city life), generosity (providing shade and cleaning the air), and beauty (a living reflection of the Creator).

Just as a single tree bears witness to certain valuable traits, so we too, as Christians, need to stand steadfast in faith, bearing witness to God's love, no matter where we are planted.

Week 2 /Day 4

MESMERIZED

I have told you these things, so that in me you may have peace. In this world you will have trouble. But take heart! I have overcome the world. John 16:33

My wife and I have been starting our mornings with short *lectio divina* sessions, during which we read a Bible passage, discuss it, and then spend a short time meditating. While day while I was meditating at a winter rental house next to a small lake, I noticed reflections of sun-lit water ripples dancing among the leaves of trees next to the shore. The constant random movement of the reflected light was mesmerizing.

I thought how much we love to look at flickering campfires or glinting sunlight off water. There is something soothing about light and random movement, and I appreciate the mystery of these encounters with the natural world without trying to figure out the "why."

Jesus said many things that must have seemed mysterious to His followers. Some of His teachings are still mysterious to us, as His life was meant to bridge the gap between the physical and the spiritual with a total understanding of each of these realms.

We see the spiritual (and even the physical with all our scientific knowledge) only through a dark glass, as Paul stated. Yet we want more. We want to know the why and how. We don't want the bad and the good experiences in our lives to seem random, yet when we try to explain them, it's usually without much success.

We cannot figure out the "why" of much of the world, but we can have the peace that passes all understanding by accepting the mystery of Jesus and being mesmerized by His love.

Week 2 /Day 5

IMPERMANENCE

Jesus Christ is the same yesterday, today, and forever. Hebrews 13:8

Our neighborhood has access to a small strip of beach along Lake Michigan's eastern shore. When my wife and I bought our house several years ago, a wide sandy beach extended 30 to 40 yards from the foot of beach grass-covered dunes to the waterline. Never having lived near one of the Great Lakes, we thought the beach was permanent. We've since found out that the changing water levels and recurring storms continually reshape the beach. Last summer there was often no more than 10 feet of beach beyond where the dunes were washing into the lake.

In reality, nothing on this Earth, or even in the universe beyond, is permanent. Whether we look back longingly, look forward hopefully, or even just try to exist in the moment—we will never experience permanence in this life. Only through faith in Christ can we anchor ourselves in the timeless love of our Lord. As the world continues to spin around us, we can remain firm in the knowledge that we too will join the timeless Lord in a place prepared beyond time.

This Coming Week

Try to do an act of kindness each day, as a way to grow the vine of Christ in the world.

Week 3 /Day 1

PROMISING SEASONS

Bless the Lord, winter cold and summer heat; sing praise to Him and highly exalt Him forever. Prayer of Azariah 45 (inserted between Daniel 3:23 and 3:24) NRSV

As the autumn days of November continued to get darker, drearier, and colder, I thought about how just three months ago summer was still in bloom although the sun was already waning. This got me to thinking how many of us living in northern areas often dread winter and its lack of sunlight.

The slow return to longer days is what characterizes the winter sun whereas the summer sun is always in decline. There is more future promise in the winter sunlight than there is in summer sunlight, which is always slipping towards shorter days.

There's a certain irony in these seasonal observations that is reflected in our Christian lives. The summer and fall of our lives are consumed with producing, growing physically, and harvesting. We are often too much in the sun with our busyness to reflect or to be concerned with spiritual matters of the soul. Our winters and early springs, however, are quieter and darker and we begin looking with anticipation to the future of new life—those times when we will be with the Lord in a summer that will never end.

Week 3 /Day 2

NOW AND LATER

Posterity will serve Him; future generations will be told about the Lord. Psalm 22:30

Jesus taught that the greatest commandments are to love God and to love our neighbor. When the righteous lawyer asked Jesus to define "neighbor" (Luke 10:29), Jesus told him the story of the Good Samaritan. In other words, don't worry about whom, when, or where; just show love. Neighbor can include just about anyone, anywhere.

Love of neighbor includes not only our contemporaries living on Earth now, but also all future people who will share this same Earth. The Bible seems to have differing takes on the long-term effects of "the sins of the fathers." We do not know how much of what we do today will have impact—positive or negative—on the physical and spiritual worlds of future generations.

It is nevertheless true that we borrow the use of God's earth from our children and our children's children. So to live within the Biblical precepts of "love thy neighbor" would mean to make sure our future neighbors have food and shelter. Our children would then be assured of a much better world. The love of God and the love of neighbor stretch from now into the rest of eternity.

Week 3 /Day 3

NOVEMBER SUNSET

The people who walked in darkness have seen a great light; those who lived in a land of deep darkness—on them light has shined. Isaiah 9:2 NRSV

I walked down to the beach along Lake Michigan at the end of another cloudy, dreary, and cold November day. Suddenly there was a break in the clouds on the western horizon just before sunset. Sunlight briefly streamed across the lake surface and suddenly illuminated the beach with a beautiful, orange-tinted light. Sand and beach grass-covered dunes appeared in a light I had ever experienced before, nor have I seen since. The effect only lasted for a few minutes before the sun set, but the fleeting transformation left a lasting impact on me.

The experience made me think of descriptions of transformations in the Bible, such as the appearance of angels described several places in the Old and New Testaments including the Transfiguration of Jesus. All short, but extremely meaningful encounters with God. I didn't immediately derive any particular meaning from my experience. However, it made me aware of how we become so accustomed to seeing the world around us in a certain way that we are shocked when suddenly the familiar takes on unfamiliarity.

I'm as guilty as anyone of getting far too familiar with my own prayer life and church attendance. My life is predictable and, frankly, sometimes boring. At those times I have little appreciation for what I should be worshiping—not some benevolent and uninspiring god, but rather the almighty powerful Lord and Creator of the Universe. He is the thrower of stars and planets across this and other universes.

To paraphrase the author Annie Dillard, if we really appreciated who God is, we should all be wearing crash helmets in church and ushers should issue life preservers and signal flares as they lash us to our pews. He's a God of love, but He is also the Creator and Transformer of the entire universe. We stand in awe.

236

Week 3 /Day 4

SURROUNDED BY LIFE

And to every beast of the earth, and to every bird of the air, and to everything that creeps on the earth, everything that has the breath of life, I have given every green plant for food. And it was so."
Genesis 1:30 NRSV

For many years, I have usually started my day with a very short prayer of thanks—thanks for my living another day, for God's love, for family, for friends, for health, and for wealth (which, by the standards of billions of people in the world, is uncomfortably large). A few weeks ago, I started thinking about also thanking God not just for my life but for the lives of everyone around me and then beyond that to the miracles of life in all living things—the trees and flowers outside the window, even the birds at the feeders.

Life fills every corner of this beautiful garden that the Lord has created. As Elizabeth Barrett Browning said, "Earth's crammed with heaven, / And every common bush afire with God; / But only he who sees, takes off his shoes, /The rest sit round it and pluck blackberries."

As part of the Trinity, Jesus is the source of all earthly life we see surrounding us (John 1:2). More importantly, Jesus has prepared the way beyond to eternal life. We have much to be thankful for and to include in our prayers.

Week 3 /Day 5

WALKING

Enoch walked with God, then he was no more, because God took him. Genesis 5:24 NRSV

At my age, walking seems to be my exercise of choice, except when the weather is good for a bike ride. A brisk walk can improve your health and stimulate your mind. Many creative artists, writers, and poets have been inspired while walking in the outdoors.

Enoch and God were obviously very close, and like old friends they could enjoy each other's company without saying a word. Enoch and God walked together 365 years, until God invited Enoch into the heavenly realm.

We are all called to walk with God, our friend for life and beyond. God apparently loves walking, as evidenced by His evening garden walks mentioned in Genesis. Jesus and the disciples walked everywhere. There must have been much teaching, sharing, and bantering that went on as they traveled through the countryside.

A common saying is "May you be covered in the dust of the rabbi." This saying comes from an ancient rabbinic teaching or *Mishnah*. Some scholars interpret this to mean to follow closely behind your teacher while you are learning. In contrast, Jesus invites us to walk and learn *beside* Him rather than *behind* Him, just as the two disciples did on their walk to Emmaus after the crucifixion (Luke 24).

A daily walk with the Lord means we treasure our relationship with Him and that we're in it for the long haul—for better or worse—until we are invited to the heavenly realm.

This Coming Week

Take a prayer walk around your neighborhood or in a nearby park. If you walk your neighborhood, pray for each household you pass. If you walk in a park, thank God for the natural beauty of the place.

Week 4 /Day 1

CYCLES

There is a time for everything, and a season for every activity under heaven: a time to scatter stones and a time to gather them. Ecclesiastes 3:5

Sandhill cranes gather by the thousands on marshes they have used for eons of time, V-shaped formations of geese wing south together, and herds of elk move together to grasslands at lower elevations. These are just a few of the great annual fall migrations of animals in the Northern Hemisphere. During these times, individual animals join others of their kind with the common goals of survival and security. These same animals will later separate from each other to establish territories, find mates, and raise young. This annual cycle of gathering and scattering is common among many animal species.

The Christian life also cycles between gathering and scattering, inward and outward. We gather for praise and worship, for mutual support, love, and accountability; and we scatter to spread the love of Christ into the world around us.

Paul emphasized the need for believers to meet together for worship and support (Hebrews 10:25). Jesus charged the disciples to go and preach the Good News to all the world (Mark 16:15). We can't survive long spiritually without regular contact with fellow believers. We can't be bearers of the Good News without leaving the safety and comfort of our Christian community and taking the light of Jesus into the world.

Week 4 /Day 2

WIND-BLOWN LEAVES ON THE PATIO

Heal me Lord, and I will be healed; save me and I will be saved, for you are the one I praise. Jeremiah 17:14

There are few trees growing near my house, but every fall I must clean out leaves that collect in the corners of the patio after a windy day. Leaves, dirt, trash, and flower petals always collect in nooks and crannies, along fences, or wherever the wind loses some of its energy.

I've discovered that the wind is a little like the Spirit in my life. Where the Spirit is active and blowing through my spiritual life, it's easier to remain uncluttered. However, those nooks and crannies in my life—the spots where I hide from the cleansing power of the Spirit—are where dirt and debris build up. This is somewhat like the book *My Heart, Christ's Home* by Robert Munger, where the owner shows his guest, Jesus, around the house, but purposely avoids the closet. Eventually, the owner finds out that only Jesus has the strength to clean out the closet. Only Christ has the power to clean up those nooks and crannies where I tend to hide things from Him.

We all have those dirty little places in our lives that we don't have the power in ourselves to clean up. That work must be turned over to the cleansing power of the Holy Spirit, who will sweep them clean and fill them with fresh air if we let Him.

Week 4 /Day 3

PURIFICATION CYCLES

As the rain and snow come down from heaven, and do not return to it without watering the earth and making it bud and flourish, so that it yields seed for the sower and bread for the eater, so is My word that goes out from My mouth; it will not return to Me empty, but will accomplish what I desire and achieve the purpose for which I sent it. Isaiah 55:10-11

In his book *Earth-Wise,* Cal DeWitt talks about the beauty of the water cycle on Earth. Water is continually condensing and falling to the ground as precipitation. It is also continually evaporating from the Earth's surface to return to the atmosphere. Pure rain and snow water our crops; fill our streams, rivers and lakes; quench our thirsts, and perform thousands of purposes in maintaining life on Earth.

Humans often abuse and pollute our precious waters with all sorts of wastes and contaminants. However, evaporation from even the most contaminated water re-enters the atmosphere purified.

The Lord promised through Isaiah that, like the rain and snow, His word of love through Scripture will also enter the messy matrix of our lives to work wonders of inspiration and hope, healing and renewal, and wisdom and guidance. When we accept that love and use it to touch others in this world, it returns in pure form to the Father despite having passed through broken and contaminated vessels.

Week 4 /Day 4

TIMING

Wait for the Lord; be strong, and let your heart take courage; wait for the Lord! Psalm 27:14

Beautiful spring wildflowers push up through the winter's leaf litter each spring in the deciduous woodlands of eastern North America. While new leaves are still forming, spring sunlight reaches the ground and warms the earth. For a few short weeks, the flowers thrive, sending up stems and leaves, blossoming, and forming seeds. The flowers then fade without a trace as the leafy tree canopy reduces light on the forest floor for another summer.

God's perfect timing is found throughout the plant and animal kingdoms where growth and reproduction depend on a narrow time frame of favorable light, temperature, and moisture conditions. Although we humans do our best to control our environments and to break away from dependence on natural cycles of abundance and scarcity, we often think we can also break away from God's timing of events in our lives. The problem is, if we get outside of God's timing, we place ourselves in danger. The Biblical advice is to be vigilant, be prepared, and wait for God to show the way.

Week 4 /Day 5

WALKING THE WRACK LINE

The seas have lifted up, Lord, the seas have lifted up their voice; the seas have lifted up their pounding waves. Psalm 93:3

Each day brings a new collection of objects washed up along the wrack line of the Lake Michigan beach near our house. Small pebbles of sandstone, quartz, and basalt—along with butterfly wings, bits of algae, and tangles of zebra mussel shells—are scattered across the sandy beach. In addition to the natural materials, there are also less-beautiful man-made flotsam and jetsam of deflated balloons, plastic bottles, cigarette butts, and small pieces of burned wood. Everything washed up along the wrack line tells a story of nature or of humankind. The constant waves are the messengers of the stories.

Prayers are like individual waves continually washing up on heaven's shore. They present the jetsam and flotsam of our lives to God as He walks the heavenly wrack line. I'm choosy in my walks along the shore. I pick up only the unusual or beautiful stone or shell ignoring the rest. But God isn't selective. God cleans the beach each day and treasurers everything brought to Him through prayer—our joys, sorrows, happiness, anger, or hurt. Some of the wrack brings Him great joy while others great pain, but everything brought to Him in prayer is treasured and will in some way be answered.

This Coming Week

Read Robert Munger's My Heart, Christ's Home.

DECEMBER DEVOTIONS

Contents:

Week 1 /Day 1

LEAF

Those who trust in their riches will fall, but the righteous will thrive like a green leaf. Proverbs 11:28

Years ago, I saw a bumper sticker that read: "Have you thanked a green plant today?" The answer for most of us is *no,* nor have we even thanked the Lord for the blessings of His green plants upon which our lives depend for food and for the very oxygenated air we breathe.

Through the miracle of sunlight-powered photosynthesis, green plants take carbon dioxide from the air and water from their roots to make sugars. Oxygen is released as a byproduct. Green leaves depend upon the sun each day to power their work; each day they are "generous" in providing food and in releasing oxygen.

We Christians need to learn how to be generous with the fruits of our labors. As in the story of the vine and the branches, we as "leaves" on the vine are an important part of God's working in the world—a work in which giving (not getting) should be a way of life.

Week 1 /Day 2

LOOKING OUT AT THE SNOW

When it snows, she has no fear for her household; for all of them are clothed in scarlet. Proverbs 31:21

As I looked out the window in late afternoon, wet, wind-driven flakes of snow blew across the gray landscape under a sullen sky. The pines whispered in the winds as their boughs swayed and caught the windblown flakes. The accumulating flakes developed a study in contrast between the deep green needles and their white frosty coating. Later, the sky cleared, and moonlight glistened on the snow.

Despite this beautiful winter scene in front of me, I was again haunted by the deep fear of cold and snow I felt as a child, worrying about somehow being left outside in the cold, even though I grew up with loving parents in a small cozy house.

My mother had many of the traits of the woman in Proverbs 31. She worked outside the home, and she was also an excellent homemaker. Yet despite my being well taken care of and always having a warm bed to sleep in, my childish fear persisted, and our family wasn't much on reading the Bible.

It wasn't until much later in life, when I started seriously reading and studying the Bible, that I finally understood how faith in the love of Jesus can cast out fear—including childish ones (1 John 4:18). Even a safe, loving family life falls short of bringing a peace that surpasses all understanding. That kind of peace only comes with a faith acknowledging that we are members of God's family.

Week 1 /Day 3

CHRISTMAS TREES

Let us make mankind in our image to be like us. Genesis 1:26 ISV

There's no mention of Trinity in the Bible, although there are allusions to it such as the one in Genesis 1:26. Another more direct reference to Trinity is in Matthew 28:19, where Jesus instructs His disciples to go and baptize in the name of the Father, the Son, and the Holy Spirit. Recognizing the "three in oneness" of God is a cornerstone of our Christian faith.

Although I've had my share of run-ins with cutting down, setting up, decorating, undecorating, and disposing of live Christmas trees, in the end, I generally enjoy them as part of the season. However, I also viewed them as one of those leftovers of paganism that got incorporated into Christianity through the centuries. Long before they were converted to Christianity, Germanic and other peoples in northern Europe celebrated winter solstice by bringing evergreen branches inside as a promise of spring.

However, at a men's Bible class I attended, one of the men mentioned that whenever he saw a Christmas tree with its generally triangular shape, he thought of the Trinity—Father, Son, and Holy Spirit. The image gave me a whole new, and much more Christ-based, view of the secular tradition of Christmas trees.

Trees of various kinds are symbolic throughout Scripture, such as the mention in Isaiah 11.1 of the shoot arising from the stump of Jesse—a reference to the Messianic line leading to Jesus. Most significantly, trees were involved in sin entering the world as well as in salvation returning to humankind. It's only natural then to think of our Christmas trees as pointing towards heaven and reminding us of our three-in-one God, who so loved the world that He gave His only begotten Son to show us the way home.

Week 1 /Day 4

THE SIGNATURE LINE

*Love the Lord your God with all your heart and with all your soul
and with all your mind and with all your strength. Mark 12:30*

I'd admit I'm not the best journal writer on a daily schedule; I often
don't have any profound insights or thoughts to write down. I may
end up skipping multiple days when I don't write anything at all.
Lately, however, I've approached journaling more prayerfully. I write
down my thoughts, no matter how mundane or trivial, in the form of
a letter to the Lord—a letter to someone I love.

When writing letters to friends and relatives, I sometimes consider
what the best closing is. Should I sign it "Blessings," "Thinking of
You," or that more powerful word, "Love"? In the case of my letters
to the Lord, there was no doubt. I needed to sign them "Love." This
simple act of signing each day's entry "love" made a difference by
reminding me to whom (and for whom) I was writing. Nothing is
mundane or trivial in the eyes of the all-encompassing Creator,
Father of our Savior Jesus and the very essence of love itself (1 John
7-18). I encourage you to write your love letter to the Lord today.

Week 1 /Day 5

COMFORT FOOD

How sweet are your words to my taste, sweeter than honey to my mouth. Psalm 119:103

On a recent cold December morning, we had a breakfast of hot, fresh-baked oatmeal with some raisins. It was real comfort food for a cold, snowy morning. The warmth, taste, consistency, and smell of these foods somehow made us feel more secure, bringing back pleasant thoughts and memories from our past.

The Bible or "Word of God" is also a spiritual comfort food for those who live in an often cold, harsh world. It reminds us that we are charged with more than just enjoying being filled with God's Word. We are also meant to feed others this comfort food, even when this means going into uncomfortable situations.

Ezekiel (Ezekiel 3:3) was told to literally "eat the scroll" with God's warning to Israel. Ezekiel tells us that the scroll was sweet as honey, but the message he had to deliver to the nation of Israel after eating it was not comfortable. Jesus refers to food as doing the will of the Father (John 4:34), and to Himself as the Bread of Life—which will sustain us, but only after His suffering on the cross. The living bread that Jesus becomes is highly fortified comfort food that gives us the strength to face the challenges of the world, the desire to spread the Good News, and the assurance of eternal life.

This Coming Week

Give prayer journaling a try. You don't need a journal to start. Any notebook (or a computer with a writing program) will work. If you have a computer or smart phone, there are prayer journal apps available to help get you started.

Week 2 /Day 1

CLARITY AT HIGHER ALTITUDES

After six days Jesus took with Him Peter, James, and John the brother of James, and led them up a high mountain by themselves. Matthew 17:1

Mountains have always played a big role in the Bible. Moses received the Ten Commandments on Mount Sinai, Elijah hid in the mountains and heard God, the Transfiguration took place on Mount Tabor, and Mount Hermon stood as a landmark throughout Biblical history.

One late winter day, my wife and I decided to hike some of the trails in the Superstition Mountains near Phoenix, AZ. As we hiked from a starting elevation of a little more than 1000 feet to about 2000 feet, we noticed the changes in the vegetation. The lower, less rocky and comparatively more moist elevation had a much greater diversity of desert plants—several cholla species, paloverde trees, saguaro cacti, barrel cacti, brittlebush, creosote bush, and ironwood trees, among others. As we climbed up the trail, the air surrounding us became cooler and quieter. The higher elevations (around 2,000 feet above sea level) showed very little plant life other than brittlebush and lichen.

The higher up the mountain, the simpler things become. With less background noise, it's easier to listen for and to hear the Lord speak. If you can visualize "climbing the mountain of God" as you pray, you may find that you also can more clearly hear His voice in the cool, quiet, thin air away from the confusion and noise of the lower altitudes.

Week 2 /Day 2

HEALING WATERS

Whoever is thirsty, let him come; and whoever wishes, let him take the free gift of the water of life. Revelation 22:17

It's well known among ecologists that deserts like the Sonoran in the Southwestern United States are more fragile and susceptible to damage than are the woodlands of the East. Vehicle tracks made in the desert may persist for decades or longer while damage from similar disturbances in wetter environments disappears in a much shorter time. A large part of the difference is due to the availability of water. Not only do the eastern woodlands receive more rainfall, they also receive it much more evenly throughout the year. Periodic deluges occur in the desert, but most of this water runs off, and then a long dry period often ensues.

Like the Eastern woodlands, consistency and regularity in the way of prayer, fellowship, and communion are necessary in our spiritual lives. The practice of these disciplines will help get us through life's hurts, frustrations, and disappointments. If we only turn to God during crises, our efforts may soon "run off" leaving us disillusioned, dry, and damaged. However, if we continually "water" our faith day in and day out with the spiritual disciplines, we are much more likely to recognize and receive the healing power of Christ in our lives.

Week 2 /Day 3

HOMING INSTINCTS

My people will abide in a peaceful habitation, in secure dwellings,
and in quiet resting places. Isaiah 32:18 NRSV

The homing and navigational instincts of many animals are truly
amazing. Monarch butterflies that mature in Canada can find their
way to their overwintering grounds among the oyamel fir forests in
Mexico's Sierra Madre Mountains. Scientists continue to be amazed
at the abilities of many migratory birds to find their way between
summer breeding and overwintering areas. Whales find their way
through the vast oceans to specific breeding and feeding areas, and
caribou migrate through hundreds of miles of tundra between
summering and wintering grounds.

God has also given us an amazing spiritual homing instinct that, if
followed, will lead us home to Him. John Wesley called it
"prevenient grace," an innate pull that we have towards a
relationship with God. We often may not even be aware of it until
some occasion in our life where, as some say, we recognize the hole
in our lives that only God can fill. This grace is a gift of the Holy
Spirit and can start us on our journey as we navigate our way with
growing faith. By realizing what Jesus has done for us and following
the path of sanctifying grace, we can find the way home.

Week 2 /Day 4

FIVE EARTHS

Your kingdom come, your will be done on Earth as in heaven.
Matthew 6:10

In thinking about the state of the world today, most Christians would agree that we're a long way from seeing the Kingdom of Heaven appearing on Earth. Embedded injustices—based largely on human selfishness and greed in our dealings with each other as individuals, groups, and nations—have created more of a hell on Earth than a Kingdom of Heaven for billions of our brothers and sisters.

The availability of resources—natural, economic, and human—is extremely skewed towards the richest nations and individuals. The Global Footprint Network estimates that it would take the equivalent of five Earths to support all of humanity to the level of an average American.

As followers of Christ and with our understanding that every person is a child of God, this inequality should concern us. But what can I do about the "structural sins" upon which governments and societies are based and in which I participate? The prophet Micah provides a guide: "seek justice, love mercy, and walk humbly with God." We all have a need to prayerfully consider our lifestyles and determine where we might be able to change some of our consumptive habits, get more involved in local issues, and show God's love to all those who share the planet with us.

Week 2 /Day 5

PALE BLUE DOT

By the word of the Lord the heavens were made, their starry host by the breath of His mouth. Psalm 33:6

Living near Lake Michigan gives me a chance to look at the night sky above 80 miles of water, without interfering lights. It reminds me of camping in the Desert Southwest and lying on a picnic table looking up at the night sky, feeling like I would fall into the universe. Such awe-inspiring and humbling experiences were the norm before we started lighting up the Earth's night with electricity.

Seeing the stars and knowing that our own galaxy is 100,000 light years across can leave you thinking and believing in one of two ways. Carl Sagan, the famous astronomer and an atheist, saw Earth as a pale blue dot suspended in a sunbeam and insignificant in the realm of the universe—a random anomaly of physical laws. However, through the eyes of faith, the psalmist in Psalm 19 sees the heavens declaring the glory of God, the skies the work of His hands.

We may be small, but God certainly has shown a special love for His little garden here among the stars—the only place we know of where life in all its diversity exists. To me, this hidden beauty of a watery, life-filled planet (this blue dot) seems very consistent with God's style. He favors the small and seemingly less significant to give Him greater glory than the large and powerful, whether stars, planets, or people.

When I look up at the night sky, I am reminded of the special place God has in His heart for the inhabitants of this pale blue dot a love so great that He sent His Son from among the stars to teach us to love.

This Coming Week

If possible, go outside on a clear night and look up at the stars. Prayerfully consider just how small we—and planet Earth—are in relationship to the universe. Remember that the God of love is also the God of the entire universe.

Week 3 /Day 1

SOARING ON THERMALS

For My yoke is easy and My burden is light. Matthew 11:30

I'm a control freak, and I know I need help. Trying to control everything that's going on in my life often drives me, and the people around me, crazy. The problem is, when you don't want to hand over any control to others, you end up overloading yourself. It takes constant effort to keep up with life.

I'm reminded of watching the mute swans taking off from the surface of a pond near our house. These large birds seem to exert tremendous effort in getting airborne, and even after they're airborne the strenuous flapping of their large wings can be heard a half mile away. It's quite a contrast to the many large hawks, seabirds, and vultures that can soar on thermals for hours while hardly moving their wings.

Control is a heavy burden that can result in alienation, fatigue, worry, depression, and even various medical problems. "Letting go and letting God" is the first step in dropping some of that heavy weight of imagined control and responsibility. Actually, are never in control. The sooner we admit it and turn our days over to God, the sooner we can soar on the thermals and stop the futile hard work of beating our wings of control.

Week 3 /Day 2

DELIGHT IN WISDOM

Four things on Earth are small, yet they are exceedingly wise . . .
Proverbs 30:24 KJV

There are over 2 million species of insects identified to date and probably a few million more still to be discovered. The abundance and diversity of insects is mind-boggling, with about 400,000 species of beetles alone living in just about every environment on Earth. Even in smaller groups like the bees there are about 20,000 species, many living solitary lives, not in hives making honey. Learning about even one aspect of one insect species can consume a lifetime of study and bring about delight in wisdom and understanding.

Insects and other animals can teach us wisdom, as mentioned in Proverbs 30 where the ants are always working together to prepare for the future; the coneys or rabbits find their shelter in protective rocks; locusts don't travel alone; and spiders can bring the beautiful symmetry of a web to light from inside themselves.

So, what are the take-aways of these small bits of wisdom? Cooperate to prepare for the future; seek the Rock for protection; don't try to travel your spiritual life alone; and when you have the inner beauty of the Lord, it will be revealed to the world!

NORTHERN LIGHTS

Out of the north He comes in golden splendor; God comes in awesome majesty. Job 37:22

Although I live in the northern Midwest, I have only seen the northern lights once. That was years ago when I was walking home from a Boy Scout meeting on a cold January night. I looked at the northern sky and saw what looked like curtains of changing light moving across the heavens. By the time I got home to tell my parents, the lights had disappeared.

The silent and fleeting beauty of Northern Lights (the *aurora borealis*) is only one small example of all the places I've experienced God's awesome majesty in nature throughout my life. In fact, part of the reason I wanted to be a biologist was because of my fascination with the incredible diversity and complexity of God's creation on this beautiful planet. I saw natural phenomena as a metaphor for spiritual reality.

Physically, the northern lights are a result of a strong solar wind (continuous streams of mostly electrons and protons emitted by the sun) encountering the Earth's magnetic field. Spiritually, God sends out a continuous flow of grace through the workings of the Holy Spirit. Through our "magnetic fields" of faith based on the spiritual disciplines of prayer, study, and service, we can intercept this flow of grace and reveal God's light and love to those around us, giving witness to God's awesome majesty.

Week 3 /Day 4

WATER CROSSINGS

And as soon as the priests who carry the ark of the Lord—the Lord of all the earth—set foot in the Jordan, its waters flowing downstream will be cut off and stand up in a heap. Joshua 3:13

Rivers can be serious impediments to movements from one place to another. Consider Exodus 14, when the Israelites fleeing the Egyptians came to the edge of the Red Sea and started to panic. Amidst the turmoil, Moses followed God's command when he held out his rod and parted the waters.

Later in the book of Joshua, the waters of the Jordan River were in spring flood when God commanded the Israelites to enter the Promised Land. The Levites stepped toward the raging river in faith, carrying the Ark of the Covenant. Because of their faith, dry ground appeared for them to safely bring the ark across.

Are you standing at the edge of something that seems to be a barrier to moving on with your life? If so, turn to the Lord in prayer as the new year approaches. Have faith. God can safely take you to the other side.

Week 3 /Day 5

NATURAL PRUNING

He removes every branch in me that bears no fruit. Every branch that bears fruit He prunes to make it bear more fruit. John 15:2 NRSV

My wife and I had just returned home to Michigan after a winter in Arizona. I noticed that there were piles of dead and broken branches beneath several of our pine trees. The piles of branches were the result of winter ice storms and wind. Soon after our return, there was a heavy, wet spring snow, and many more pine branches, both living and dead, broke off under the weight of the snow. This was a sort of natural pruning: removing dead, unproductive limbs as well as other weak limbs from the pines.

We too have a lot of dead and weakened limbs that contribute nothing to our spiritual growth. We cling to desires for wealth, fame, power, and the things of this world. It's often in the winters of our lives that we recognize the impediment these worldly desires are on our spiritual lives. These are the times when the Holy Spirit prunes us for a fuller life—a life without the burden of dead wood.

This Coming Week

Make God's wisdom a prayer focus for this week. Wisdom is based on knowledge but is more than knowledge. It is applying knowledge using insights into seeing a bigger picture.

Week 4 /Day 1

HIKING EQUIPMENT

Therefore keep watch for you know not the day or the hour.
Matthew 25:13

Last winter, my wife and I decided to take a little day hike up into the Superstition Mountains east of Phoenix. Although it was a relatively short hike, it involved a climb of around 800 feet in elevation. We had forgotten our hiking sticks, but the trail was heavily traveled, and it looked like a fairly easy walk. However, as we climbed higher, the trail became rougher, and we found ourselves scrambling over large boulders. The climb was a lot more difficult without a hiking stick to assist with our balance.

Having the right equipment even for a short hike in the desert is important. Trail signs often warn hikers to wear proper footgear, to take along adequate water, and to use a hiking stick. In our spiritual walk, we also need the right equipment. We need the "map" provided by God's Word; the "footgear" provided by spiritual disciplines such as prayer, fasting, and study; "living water" provided through worship and sacraments; and a "hiking stick" of forgiveness and hospitality to help us up and over the tough terrain.

Jesus spoke many parables to the people about being prepared for the Kingdom of Heaven and for the return of the Son of God. In the parable of the ten virgins (Mt. 25:1-13), Jesus admonishes His followers not to be foolish like five virgins who took no extra supply of oil for their lamps. Our job as the Lord's servants is to prepare properly and watch not only for Jesus's return but also for the breaking through of the Kingdom of God in our lives and of those around us through the workings of the Holy Spirit.

Week 4 /Day 2

SHAGBARK HICKORY

For He will hide me in his shelter in the day of trouble; He will conceal me under the cover of his tent; He will set me high on a rock. Psalm 27:5

Shagbark hickories are common trees throughout the Midwest. As a kid roaming the woods of western Ohio, I noticed these trees with their shaggy bark were easy to identify, even in the winter. Sometimes in autumn I would gather the hickory nuts from beneath these trees and spend hours cracking them and extracting the nutmeat for a hickory nut cake that Mom would bake.

I didn't know until much later that shagbarks were important summer homes and nurseries of now-endangered Indiana bats. Indiana bats range throughout the East and Midwest where they hibernate in the relatively few caves or old mine shafts that have the right combinations of temperature and humidity. In the spring and summer, the bats disperse to wooded areas, where they roost under the loose bark of hickories and other trees. Up to 100 female bats, each with their single yearly offspring may roost in one tree.

Christians seek God's shelter and comfort from life's trials and tribulations through our belonging to the Body of Christ, the church. While the Lord comforts us as individuals in our difficulties, there is additional comfort in praying and worshiping together as part of a fellowship of believers who support one another. The church is our shagbark hickory, where God's protecting presence is felt among the communion of saints.

Week 4 /Day 3

SIGNS OF THE SEASON

There is a time for everything and a season for every activity under heaven. Ecclesiastes 3:1

Late in January I start listening for the first cooing of the mourning doves as they respond to the slight lengthening of daylight. In my journal, I note the date, and I count my hearing the doves as the first sign of spring. It is one way I mark the changing seasons.

The Bible refers to the changing seasons in our spiritual lives. In Job, chapters 38 and 39, he recounts how God informed him of seasonal changes within the natural world and of His care for creatures of unknown to any human (Job Chapters 38 and 39). In Mark, Jesus refers to the budding fig tree as a sign of the coming summer (13:28).

As Christians, we too should be mindful of the seasons of life since we are "like the grass, and quickly fade" (Psalm 103:15). Just as there are signs of spring in mid-winter, Christians can be signs of the Kingdom of God in a world still wrapped in darkness. As with the mourning doves and lengthening days, we see the Light of the Kingdom of Heaven, and it is our calling to sing out the Good News to the world around us.

Week 4 /Day 4

CAMPFIRES

Peter was hurt because Jesus asked him the third time, "Do you love me?" He said, "Lord, you know all things, you know that I love you." Jesus said, "Feed my sheep." John 21:17

What is it about a campfire that mesmerizes us? Flames of ever-changing colors and shapes, crackling firewood, the warmth and wafting smoke all somehow can hold our attention. It can also slow our thinking, which allows us to ignore any competing thoughts. During such contemplative moments, we can sometimes see the various aspects of our lives with new clarity.

In John 21:9, Jesus built a fire along the shore before He called the disciples in from fishing. It was around this campfire and a shared breakfast of fish and bread that Peter was reconciled to Jesus after his denials the night of Jesus's arrest. It was a campfire of healing.

The late Cardinal Joseph Bernadin stated in one of his homilies delivered to a group of scouts that we are called as Christians to build "kingdom campfires": campfires kindled by the Holy Spirit and fueled by Christ's love that will warm, comfort, and nourish the hurting world around us. It's up to us to decide where we can best start kingdom campfires. It could be lit for a lonely neighbor, a hungry child, a homeless person, or someone who is depressed. Look around, there are plenty of good places to set a kingdom campfire— one that will not only comfort others but that will also help us see ourselves in the light of Christ's love.

Week 4 /Day 5

LOOKING BACK

I will remember the deeds of the Lord: yes, I will remember your miracles of long ago. I will consider all your works and meditate on all your mighty deeds. Psalm 77: 11-12

I went for a walk after a recent, wet snow that was accompanied by a strong east wind. As I walked eastward down a nearby two-track framed in drooping hemlocks, most of the tree branches were green. It was when I turned around to look back that I saw a winter wonderland. Each branch and needle was coated in white.

The Israelites often were told to look back and see what God had done for them. The Book of Deuteronomy is often referred to as "the book of looking back and moving forward." The last book of the Torah, it reviews much of what God had already done for the Israelites and the guidance through the law that they had been given.

My wife and I often discuss how sometimes it so much easier to see how God has worked in our lives when we look back over our time together. A clearer understanding of where we have been can guide us into the future. Whether we look back and see blessings or difficulties, we can have confidence that God will lead us to a closer walk with Him if we just ask.

This Coming Week

Make a resolution to walk closer to the Lord throughout the coming year.